I HEAR VOICES

A DESCENT INTO THE DARK HALF OF PSYCHOTIC KILLER, HERBERT MULLIN

RYAN GREEN

For Helen, Harvey, Frankie and Dougie

Disclaimer

This book is about real people committing real crimes. The story has been constructed by facts but some of the scenes, dialogue and characters have been fictionalised.

Polite Note to the Reader

This book is written in British English except where fidelity to other languages or accents are appropriate. Some words and phrases may differ from US English.

Copyright © Ryan Green 2024

All rights reserved

ISBN: 9798340116178

YOUR FREE BOOK IS WAITING

From bestselling author Ryan Green

There is a man who is officially classed as "**Britain's most dangerous prisoner**"

The man's name is Robert Maudsley, and his crimes earned him the nickname "**Hannibal the Cannibal**"

This free book is an exploration of his story...

★★★★★   "*Ryan brings the horrifying details to life. I can't wait to read more by this author!*"

Get a free copy of **Robert Maudsley: Hannibal the Cannibal** when you sign up to join my Reader's Group.

www.ryangreenbooks.com/free-book

CONTENTS

Save The World 7
Son of Man 19
Spiral 25
Rebirth 40
Samsara 58
Escaping Karma 72
I Am Become Death 91
The Testament 98
After the End 113
Want More? 130
Every Review Helps 131
About Ryan Green 132
More Books by Ryan Green 133
Free True Crime Audiobook 138

Save The World

Sweat trickled down into Herb's eyes as he drove along. A sharp salty sting that grounded him in his body and brought him back to the physical world.

Being the leader of a generation was not easy. Being a transcendent soul in a world of mud and filth and confusion was the hardest thing anyone had ever had to do. Nobody else seemed to understand. Even when he lowered himself to their level and spoke to them with words from this meat, rather than allowing the natural telepathy that connected all people to speak for him, they simply did not comprehend. Sometimes he'd meet someone and there would be a glimmer of understanding, a spark of hope, but they'd soon dash it given a bit of time. They'd fall back into the dirt, lose sight of the divine self that existed above this morass of mortality, and turn away from him as if afraid that his light shining so bright might blind them.

Herb didn't hate them for that. He was too enlightened for hate. He had ascended far past the point of hate. Hate was banal. It was a thing for the common meat people, not for bright souls such as himself. He looked down with pity upon those who shied away from the brilliance of what he was becoming. He felt sorrow when they drifted away or tried to chain him down to the corporeal world. He reasoned that it must be similar to what a pet's owner might feel when the beast bit the hand that fed it. They were doing it out of ignorance, not malice. They were blinded to the true reality because they simply could not perceive the same wavelengths as him. That wasn't their fault. Not really.

Learning about the world beyond their limitations was scary for people still stuck in the meat world. Still bound to flesh already decaying. They rejected it, not because it wasn't true, but because if it was true then they'd have to give up so many of the lies that their world was built on. They'd have to give up consumerism and greed. They'd have to give up self-worship and self-obsession. All the foundations that society was built on were based on the petty concerns of this world, and if you took those foundations away, all their castles would come tumbling down. So Herb didn't take any personal offence, he just felt sorry for them.

His family, his friends, everyone he'd ever known, even the ones he'd studied with, had all hit a wall eventually. His was a wisdom too hard for them to process. A plateau they could not ascend above. His parents, to Herb's way of thinking, were small-minded people devoted to keeping him ignorant so that they could maintain their sense of superiority. When he had come to them with the truth they'd shied away, tried to lock him up, denying him his voice and his freedom. But nothing would stop him; he would let people know. Oh yes. He would let them know the truth. He was the leader of this generation and though they had tried to hobble him by keeping him ignorant, his wisdom had shone through. He had pierced the veil of wool they tried to pull over his eyes. He could do anything now. He was a grown man. A wise man. Learned, not just in the ways of this world, but in the ways of other worlds too, higher worlds. Better worlds.

When he'd told them that he could hear their thoughts, they had challenged him. When he'd told them word for word what they were thinking, they had pretended that he was just making it all up. They denied their own thoughts rather than letting him know the extent of his astonishing progress. How could he be making it up? He was hearing their voices. He heard his father, brimming with pride at the sight of his enlightened son, thinking that he hoped that someday, when the time was right, Herb would be the one to kill him. But even though he could hear him, even though he knew that in his heart his father was delighted, out loud his parents had stayed committed to upholding the status quo. They were both agents of the system, dedicated members of the web of unbelievers that held humanity down and stopped it from ascending. Even when they were actively thinking about how glorious Herb's growth had been, their words, the words they forced out of their mouths, were denying it.

They were a part of this meat world, tools of this tawdry material society that meant to stop him from developing his consciousness. That was why they had always denied him what he needed. Why they had threatened him with imprisonment and worse when he sought out the chemistry needed to open up his mind and hear the voice of the universe. But now he was saving their lives whether they believed it or not. He was born for this moment, to use his knowledge of the greater universe for a grand purpose.

Humanity.

They might not have believed in him, but he believed in them. He knew that they could rise from this pitiful state to be like him. He knew that they could become enlightened. Ascendant souls, breaking free of the shackles of the flesh to become so much more than they had ever dreamed of. The cosmos sang to him in his sleep. The voices of the world whispered their wisdom to him when he woke. Every mind was open to him, telling him the secret truths that the waking world of dreamers would deny. He knew, without having to be told, just how desperately people were searching for meaning and purpose in their shallow, pointless lives. The kind of meaning and purpose that only he could provide them. He was their leader, and he would lead from the front. He would follow the path to ascension and master the gifts that the cosmos had bestowed upon him. He would rise, and with his rising, all would be ascendant. Just as a rising tide lifted all ships, a rising soul would enlighten all around it. Once they had moved past the world of illusions and heard his mind in theirs, there would be no more hesitation, there would be no more confusion. They just needed to rise that little bit beyond where they lay trapped to realize that the keys to their shackles had been in their hands all along. All they needed to do was hear him. His voice would lead them out of the darkness and into the light.

Everything was so easy now. There was no struggle, no confusion. He knew exactly what he was meant to be doing because he was already doing it. He was listening to the voice of the cosmos guiding him forward, leading him from one place to the next, from one part of the great ritual that would save the world and bring about ascension, to whatever other challenges he would need to conquer.

An unenlightened mind would have felt the vibrations rattling through his car as he sped along through the Santa Cruz mountains and would have deemed those vibrations meaningless. A simple side effect of the internal combustion engine powering the vehicle. But Herb knew better. He was a part of the global consciousness, he was ascendant, and he knew that vibrations were everything. The heartbeat of reality.

These vibrations weren't coming from the car's engine, and they weren't a bit of roughness in the road being translated into a rumble by the wheels. They emanated from the earth beneath the tarmac. The earth was screaming out for revenge at how the world had been exploited and mutilated to serve the mainstream human culture. It wanted vengeance for how channels had been carved into Mother Earth's beautiful face and cauterised with hot tar all so these monstrous machines, burning dead dinosaur bones, could tear around pumping out poison gas for no better reason than to make more money for those that already had money.

Mother Earth was crying out for retribution. For blood. She wanted death on a grand scale, and she could have it quite easily. Beneath the tarmac and the dirt and the rocks there were fault lines here in California. Deep fault lines that would require little more than one shrug from Mother Nature and she could slough off every human being in the entire state straight into the sea. She wanted to do that. The universe wanted it to happen. The state was full to bursting with people who had sinned against nature. People who had sinned against Herb, denying him his rights and his path to glory. People who would fight tooth and nail to preserve a world in which there was so much misery and suffering when they could simply let go of their attachments and exist in a state of blissful freedom. Even though these people tried to rebel against him and make themselves into his enemies, Herb would not allow it. He would not allow himself to hate, because he was too enlightened. Hate was for them, not for him. He chose the better path, the path of forgiveness, and the path of heroism. They would all die if Mother Nature was left to her own devices, but with an enlightened soul in the world, there was another way. The earth did not need to shake and tremble. Their towers of avarice did not need to fall, dooming countless innocents to death just because they had been taken in by the big lie. They could be preserved, and in lengthening their lives, Herb could grant them the chance to experience true freedom.

In death, they would merely move on to the next cycle, they would not advance, they would not progress. They would be trapped yet again by the same deceptions, the same distractions, the same mistakes. They would be doomed to repeat this incarnation over and over until they finally recognized that living like this was fundamentally wrong, that a spiritual path was the only way out of the pointless rut they had been mindlessly excavating their entire lives and every life they'd previously experienced. He could keep them here just a bit longer, keep them in this cycle, safe and sound so that they might learn from him so that they too might ascend and grow and become all that they were meant to be. Everything that the cosmos wanted them to be – everything they were thus far failing to be.

Mother Nature had to be appeased, he had to feed Her and spill blood for Her, like the cultures of old. They knew Her under the mask of their gods and goddesses, but they also knew that sacrifice was required to keep Her wrath at bay. Her wrath, which he could feel even now, was simmering beneath the surface, beneath the soil, pounding on the periphery of his mind. She was so angry at what mankind had become. So furious at their failings. Back when people recognized her power and routinely offered sacrifice to her, that wrath, partly assuaged, had destroyed a city or two here and there. Should she unleash her long-neglected rage now, she might very well shuck the entire human race off her surface.

Herb had to keep that from happening. He had to keep her at bay until mankind could learn its lessons and grow. He was the only one who could hear her. The only one who had ascended enough that his natural telepathy extended beyond the voices of all the people around him to encompass the voice of the whole planet. The voice of the cosmos, it was more distant still, but the voice of the world was deafeningly loud and boomed at him from every direction. It was going to kill. The world was going to kill. It was going to kill and kill. It would never stop. And there was nothing that all the money, all the technology, and all the rest of the pointless nonsense mankind wasted its time on could do to stop her once she started. The only thing that could be done was for Herb to stop the slaughter before it could start.

It had been a long drive out here, but he could still hear the voice calling him, leading him on like a beacon. All he had to do was follow that voice and he'd find what he needed. He'd find that which would prevent the tragedies to come. The universe was guiding him. He could hear it. He could feel it like a magnetic pull in his bones.

And then, that beacon shone through, cutting through the dim twilight of the material world, illuminating him in the voice that had been guiding him here all this time.

"Me. It is me."

There by the side of the road, rambling along, was a homeless man. Herb didn't judge those who chose to live like nomads. He was something of a nomad himself. He didn't think that owning material things like a house made you important, he didn't think that owning anything at all made you important. You were born with your brightly burning soul and you either had grace or you didn't. You couldn't buy it. You couldn't... he was getting distracted. He listened again for the voice.

"It is me that you are looking for," The old man in his rear-view mirror whispered to him telepathically, "It is me that you have been seeking to prevent the catastrophe."

Herb pulled up at the side of the road, the homeless man still idling along towards him, just out of sight. This was where he was meant to be. This was what he was meant to do. Finally, it was all coming together. Finally, he would be able to do the thing that he had been sent to this world to do.

Setting the scene. He needed something that would make sense and could draw the homeless man closer. Herb was in a car, so he could pretend to have car trouble. Easy, simple. The simplest solution was the best one. It had elegance. He got out onto the tarmac and went to the front of the car, opened the bonnet, propped it open and stared inside. The shapes inside held no meaning for Herb, he didn't understand them. He knew that the engine worked, but he didn't know how. Didn't know what he could claim was wrong. This was a thing of the material world, a tawdry indicator of wealth and station, he had no use for it, but at this moment, he wished that he had at least some knowledge of it. Something to help him lie convincingly. Even though it ran completely contrary to his nature to lie.

If the world was as it should be, then there would have been no need to lie, but in a world full of liars, there was no other option. Even though the man walking to him even now had summoned him, called out to him across the world with his telepathy, brought him here for them to share the moment together that was soon to come, if he spoke to the man about it, the man would lie. He would claim that he did not send Herb a telepathic summons. He would claim that he did not want what his mind was screaming out to Herb that it wanted. These people, these poor people, they were so entangled in the material world that they couldn't even think clearly. They couldn't know their own thoughts or the messages that they were projecting. They had lived among the lies and the liars for such a long time that they didn't know anything else. It was another tragedy that Herb had been blind to until his enlightenment had arrived, and now it hurt his soul every single time that he encountered it. It was so unfair. It was so unfair that people knew in their hearts exactly what they needed to happen, but they couldn't express themselves with their words, only with their telepathy. It had confused Herb so much in the beginning when he was first coming into his powers as a leader of mankind. Now the pain was like an old friend, familiar and dulled with its repetition.

The man was coming closer now, still trudging along with the same dogged determination that had brought him out this far. Like a pilgrim on a holy journey, his weary legs brought him closer and closer to the divine. Herb waited, still staring down into the arcane machinery that he could not even begin to understand. It was a microcosm of the world, Herb staring into the complex machinery that meant nothing to him and mattered even less, just waiting for the moment when enlightenment might arrive. Not enlightenment about the machine, no, he still had no interest in that. But the greater enlightenment. The awareness of his higher purpose. It was like this when he was first starting out. Back when he was just learning his purpose and place in the cosmos. When he would be waiting there, just waiting, with his mind open, for inspiration to strike. For wisdom to come strolling up the road and arrive. It was so close now that he could almost taste it. He wasn't imagining the sound of the tramping steps in the gravel by the roadside. He wasn't imagining the constant keening sound of the other man's telepathic pleading with him. "Do it. Please do it. It is the only way for the world to be safe. It is the only way to be sure that there will be a future for mankind. Without you, we are all doomed. You must perform the ritual. You must appease the hungering earth. I beg you. Do what you need to. It is my purpose to be here. It is my purpose to help you in fulfilling yours. You are the leader of this generation. The master of our souls."

Herb's hands shook as he clung to the grill of the car. Sending vibrations through the great machine that had fallen silent and still after he'd turned the keys. The man was approaching. Watching him with great interest. He had to keep his eyes downturned. If their gazes met, then his own telepathy might give too much away, and even though this man wanted in his soul to help save the world, that did not mean that in his waking mind, he would understand. Herb was too powerful, his thoughts too forceful, he projected them out into the minds of all around him, and sometimes, just sometimes, those around him were sensitive enough to hear them.

The man's voice sounded different when it came from his mouth instead of through telepathy. The accent was different. The cadence and roughness. "Having car troubles, friend?"

And so his fate was sealed and Herb knew that this was the right course to follow. He had called him a friend. He was a friend to the leader of mankind. The leader of the generation. He had named himself a friend to the cause, and he would willingly sacrifice everything that he was, abandoning this cycle of his life so that others might live on. So that Herb could teach them so that they too could ascend. All it had taken was that one word, and Herb had known that despite the differences between the telepathic beacon and the voice that he heard now, things were proceeding as they were meant to. The future was his for the saving, all thanks to this wonderful new friend that he had made.

The rambling pilgrim stepped up beside Herb without invitation and peered down into the shadowed recess of the car. He sniffed the air, as though by scent alone he could diagnose whatever had brought Herb's car to its unplanned halt. Then he declared, "Reckon it needs more oil. You got some?"

There could have been no better set-up. No easier way to move forward. Herb nodded his head, not in answer to the man's spoken question, but in answer to the one that echoed in his mind through their telepathic link. "Will you do it? Will you save the world? Will you make my purpose complete?"

Still saying nothing, Herb walked around to the trunk of the car and popped it open. If you could not hear the telepathic communication, then you might have assumed that he was going to get the oil that the man had prescribed for his perfectly healthy car. Another microcosm of the greater whole that was this ruined world. Medicine for machines that were not sick.

From out of the trunk he drew a baseball bat, another product, another purchase, another part of the broken world, but one that had been designed with a purity of purpose, a purity of form. It was a thing made for one purpose, a divine instrument of sorts. Whittled down from a greater single piece of wood into this perfection that he held before him now. Wood, but shaped by steel. Shaped not by a craftsman's hands as it should have been, but by a machine. Another microcosm. A divine instrument, made without love, care, or art. A tree had died so that it could be made, and the ones who had consigned it to death had not even thought twice about it. Had not even cared enough to whittle it down from tree to divine instrument for themselves, entrusting that task to some mindless automation. It was everything that was wrong with the world, but in Herb's hands, it would make things right. It would bring peace. It would soothe the thrumming heart of Mother Earth below. He would bring peace. He was a divine instrument. Whittled from a precious innocent soul into a creature that could survive in this world, but he too maintained his purity. His purity of purpose. He would swing, and he would strike, and all the force that could be brought to bear by the cosmos would be brought through him. Focused down to the single point of contact with the tawdry material world, right here where he stood. He would strike like a bolt of lightning. He would be the cure, the medicine for a sickness that the people in their great and wicked machine did not even know that they had contracted.

Herb paced around the car with the bat held low at his waist, hidden from sight, just as he had been hidden from sight until this final moment. But soon would come the revelation. Soon would come the sacrifice, and the spilling of blood, and the peace within the rumbling heart of the world. He would do this because it was his purpose. He would do this because, throughout his entire sojourn around the car, the voice of the pilgrim still whispered in his mind. "I am a temporary vessel for a fragment of the divine, and by setting me free, you are saving millions of lives. There need be no shame in this, no sorrow, because my life was always going to end here by the side of this road. I have travelled long and hard to reach this sacred site. This holy land. Where I shall meet the instrument of divinity and perform my part. Free me from this mortal form, Herb. I beg you. You are the only one who can set me free. The only one that can save mankind. You are our leader. Our Master. Our Saviour. Praise you. Praise be to you Herb Mullin, for you are the chosen one who will save us all. You are the most beloved of the cosmos, born sacred."

He closed the final few steps, and still, the pilgrim did not look up from the engine. Only muttering to himself, "Don't look like the radiator's overheating."

Athleticism had once been Herb's domain. But now he believed that strength of arms was a failing, not a virtue. In that moment he had all the power that he needed to raise the bat and swing with all his strength. He had been granted that strength from on high. And the world would be saved at that moment when bat met skull and a crack like thunder sounded out across the abandoned hillside

Son of Man

On April 18th, 1947, Herbert Mullin was born in Salinas, Monterey County, California. While it was an entirely normal birth to an entirely normal family, it is important to note two things about that date. The first was that it occurred exactly forty-one years after the 1906 San Francisco Earthquake, an occasion notable for its horrific death toll. The second was that it was the same day in the year that the scientist Albert Einstein would eventually pass away in 1955. While these two facts may seem to be entirely unrelated to one another, Herb would feel in later life that the date of his birth was extremely significant to who he was as a person, and what his purpose in the world would be.

The Mullin family was quiet, conservative, and religious. The father, Martin, was a veteran of the Second World War, and while he was never abusive to his children, he was considered to be a very stern man, even for that particular moment in history. He did show his son affection where he could, though. He shared stories with him about his experiences in the war, taught him how to fire a gun, and even engaged in playful boxing matches with the young boy in the kitchen while their dinner was being cooked.

All of these things would be warped in Herb's mind as he grew older. The playful shadow-boxing with his father became lethal challenges set forth by a sadist, the tales of his father's time in the war intended to inflict on the boy the same traumas as his father had suffered, and his education in the use of weapons became a prelude to tricking the boy into suicide. But all of these bizarre accusations came much later, long after the events had passed from everyone else's memories, and at the time, Herb seemed to be happy and thriving.

Herb's mother, Jean, was an extremely devout Catholic who would hear no question about her beliefs. Martin was as stern a father as anyone could imagine, but even he considered her to be overzealous, particularly when it came to the education of the children. She portrayed the outside world, the secular world, as a dangerous and unhappy place where anything could happen, and she was insistent upon bringing the children to church every Sunday so that they could receive communion and be forgiven for their myriad sins.

Unfortunately for everyone involved, Herb Mullin was intelligent. Painstakingly, sharply, intelligent.

The aphorisms that his mother and father shared as though they were wisdom were easily broken down into their component parts by the boy, and he soon found what he considered to be massive deception being played out against him. The communion wafer in particular was a sticking point for him. Though he was taught that through the power of God, it transformed from simple bread into the body of Christ, he refused to believe it. He palmed his wafer, broke it apart and examined it for any traces of meat – human or otherwise. He debated the subject with his mother, who in her devotion to her Catholic faith found that she had no other recourse but to punish him for his blasphemous statements. And with that punishment, the spark of rebellion in the little boy was stoked. He had discovered the truth about the world, and he was being punished for it? So began the conspiratorial thinking that would consume him in the coming years, even if it had not yet fully developed into mental illness.

The first conspiracy that Herb came to believe in was that his parents were deliberately trying to prevent him from forming friendships. He didn't know why, precisely, beyond a general sense of malevolence from them that had been expressed through his punishment for blasphemous questions. Regardless, he quite firmly believed that the reason he could not freely approach any adult in the neighbourhood and strike up a pleasant conversation had nothing to do with the fact that he was a small and often awkward child, and everything to do with his parents having gone around, door to door, asking people to ignore him. From his perspective, it was the only logical reason that he was ignored in this manner, and he convinced himself that he had seen the adults in his life conversing with the other neighbours when he wasn't around. There was clearly something going on that he was being deliberately excluded from. Some secret that he wasn't privy to.

His attempts to investigate his parent's meddling were thwarted by their constant oversight, and later, by an entirely unexpected uprooting when they moved to San Francisco. It was a world apart from the relative quiet of the farming town that he'd grown up in, a place of dazzling lights and constant motion that was entirely alien to the boy. He withdrew into himself, initially out of fear, but soon another seismic shift occurred in his life. At the age of five, having been hauled away with barely a moment's notice, he began attending school.

Almost immediately he was recognized as being uncommonly bright for a boy his age, but unlike many of the other children who were tarred with the brush of great potential, Herb was well-liked by his peers, making friends easily, with a gentle nature that seemed at odds with his precise and analytical mind.

His father quickly assimilated into their new life and found work as a furniture salesman in the city. Herb's older sister, who attended the same school as Herb, struggled considerably more with having been uprooted from her established group of friends. Such a marked contrast between the siblings only made Herb appear better in the eyes of his teachers. Making friends and gaining popularity came as easily to Herb as academic success, and he soon found himself as a leader among his classmates, both in the classroom and out on the playing field where he began establishing himself as a competent athlete from a very young age.

Unfortunately, many of his mother's prophecies about the dark and dangerous secular world seemed to be proven true after their arrival in San Francisco. He had lived an extremely sheltered life before, with his knowledge of the world carefully limited by his parents to ensure that he was not tempted to sin. Living among the children of a metropolis resulted in an entirely different viewpoint and given that Herb already had his parents framed as antagonists in his mind, it didn't take long before he started finding fault in everything that they did. The other children in his class were the result of more liberal parents, and physical affection between parent and child was common in their households. This led to a great deal of confusion for Herb, who began to interpret his parent's more restrained nature as disgust with him. Unfortunately, he also became aware of sex at the same age. Listening in on the conversations of older students, Herb began to conflate sexual contact with the kind of acceptable parental contact that he might have expected. He came to believe that his father's disinterest in sexually assaulting him stemmed from a hatred of him, and a wish to deny him pleasure. A pleasure that he felt certain all the other boys in his class were receiving from their own fathers. He would later claim that the blame for the majority of the missteps that he made in later life could be laid at his father's feet because the adult man had neglected to perform oral sex on his six-year-old son.

He did not discuss any of this with his peers out of shame that his father's lack of affection for him might be discovered.

Instead, Herb went through much of his young life believing that his father did not love him as evidenced by the absence of thoroughly inappropriate physical contact.

Ironically, all of this exposure to the lifestyles that his parents were trying to keep him away from actually happened at a parochial Catholic school. A place that by the standards of the city was intensely conservative and safe from outside influences.

School was a very easy time in Herb's life. Perhaps the last time that he was truly happy. He was effortlessly passing all of his classes, reigning champion of the various sports that he indulged in, and had the sort of social life that would have been the envy of anyone. Mentally, he attributed all of this to the fact that he managed to get to all of the kids at school before his parents could turn them against him. Now that they were in a bigger city, his father's reach was limited by the unfamiliar terrain and the much larger population. It would be so much more difficult to conduct their conspiracy in such a place, even if he did sometimes see them talking to other adults that he didn't know without including him.

He continued through school with nothing but success under his belt until the middle of high school, when another change of jobs for Martin precipitated another move for the family. At least, that was the reasoning that was given to Herb. In reality, his mother had been extremely unhappy living in the city, which she considered to be brimming with vice and sin. She correctly deduced that her son's newfound reticence when talking to his parents was a result of his being led astray, though she never quite grasped just how far astray Herb had wandered.

Their new home was Felton, a little town planted among the majestic redwoods of Santa Cruz County which was as picturesque as it was isolated from the outside world. From the perspective of his parents, it was an ideal solution to the exposure to secular culture that Herb had suffered. There wasn't a parochial school available for him, but they considered the isolation and quiet of the town to be more than sufficient protections for their son.

Herb actually proved to fit in just as well in Felton as he had back in the city, arriving with the added mystique of a big-city boy to get him over the initial awkwardness of having to start over again socially.

This fresh start actually turned out to be a great thing for Herb. He had smoothed off all his rough edges at his last school and could now make a first impression all over again, not as the confused child that he'd been, but as the mature and well-put-together teenager that he'd become. For the most part, his conspiratorial obsessions and the distress from his early life had been put behind him and he had grown into the persona that he had constructed for himself. He was a star athlete, popular, top of all his classes, and beloved by essentially everyone. He still had some minor problems with trusting authority figures but he had learned to couch his concerns in language that made it less of a conflict and more of an exploration of alternate approaches.

Hormones were also thoroughly kicking in at this point, and the casual ease that Herb had always had when talking to girls suddenly became a massive asset. He was already one of the more desirable bachelors in his class because of his social status, but the fact that he was charming and being raised in a conservative family meant that he was unlikely to be pushy when it came to romance – which made him a prize catch. It should come as no surprise that he acquired a steady girlfriend very early into his time at Felton High.

In the final two years of high school, Herb found some of the closest friends that he'd ever make in his life, settled into what had all the appearances of a happy relationship, and was voted by his peers to be the "most likely to succeed." With college prospects opening up before him and decisions to make, Herb had a bright future ahead of him.

A bright future that would be abruptly snuffed out.

Spiral

Dean Richardson was Herb's closest friend in school, and in 1965 when the pair of them graduated, it looked like they'd be going on to college together too. Herb planned to study engineering, Dean didn't seem to have a particularly clear vision of what he wanted to do with his future, apart from picking up girls on his rad new motorbike. But the trajectory of both young men's lives changed when a car struck Dean's motorbike, sending it careening out across the road and ultimately killing him.

In reality, this was probably the first real trauma that Herb had ever encountered in his life. He had been born with some mental instability; that much is clear from the bizarre way that he often thought about things even as a child, but so long as he had been kept insulated from anything too terrible, he had been able to persist as a normal and functioning member of society. There was a fragility to his sanity, but so long as nothing came along and jostled it, he could likely have proceeded through his whole life without ever having it truly broken.

The death of Dean was a breaking point for Herb. Almost overnight, his bedroom was converted into a vast shrine dedicated to his dead friend. His plans for the future were cast aside as he devoted himself exclusively to mourning. His relationship with his girlfriend came to an abrupt end when she complained about his obsessive behaviour over some dead boy, and he informed her that he was becoming a homosexual. That it was the only logical explanation for his fixation on his dead friend, obviously he had been in love with him. As far as Herb was concerned, there was no other imaginable reason why he might have such a heightened response to the boy's death otherwise.

This was essentially the first time that Herb had needed to deal with the concept of death, and when confronted with existential terror for the first time, he did what many people do and sought out comfort in religion. Unfortunately for him and his parents, the religions that he sought comfort in were far from the Catholicism that he had been raised in and that he mistrusted so deeply. Instead, Herb began studying Eastern religions, as many of the youth of America did in this time period, and given his recent trauma he latched on to the concept of reincarnation very strongly. The idea that his friend was not dead, but had simply moved on to a new life somewhere else in the world was far less upsetting to Herb. The concept of reincarnation became something of an obsession for him, almost as intense as his fixation on Dean. But he still felt like he didn't have the full breadth of understanding. While there were popular translations of many of the Eastern religious texts available in America by the 1960s feeding into the growing counter-culture, access to more academic translations was considerably more limited, and as such it soon became apparent to Herb that if he wanted to learn more about the philosophy and religion of the other side of the world, then he would have to physically travel there.

Shockingly, his parents were not in favour of this idea. Neither the idea of their cloistered teenage son travelling to Asia nor the idea of them funding his trip over there to indulge in the study of what one of them considered to be Satanic and the other considered to be barbarous savagery. They would not be assisting him with his desire to make a pilgrimage to the East and learn more about reincarnation, nor would they continue to support him while he lay about the house moping all the time. It was long past the point that he should have moved on from his friend's death. Long past the point that he should have been putting his affairs in order and getting back to either college or the workforce.

Another option was floated by his father. The military. It would make a man out of the boy, give him some discipline and push those foolish thoughts about religion and spirituality right out of his head.

Enlistment became a much-debated subject in the Mullin household in the years following Dean's death, as did Herb's detachment from reality. It is likely that both parents already suspected the worst about their son and believed that if he did attempt to join the armed forces, his issues would be revealed early on by the various medical assessments Herb would undergo. Such examinations might prove his parents' longstanding belief that there was something wrong with Herb's mind, or maybe that he had been abusing drugs. Either would have resulted in his immediate dishonourable discharge, so the issue was never pressed.

In truth, Herb had begun experimenting with drugs shortly after the death of his best friend. He used marijuana to help calm himself when he was slipping into bouts of anxiety, but ultimately slowed his consumption of the herb when he realized just how badly it was dampening his mental faculties. He was the most likely to succeed, the smartest kid in the room, he couldn't be all that while also indulging in enough marijuana to render him little more than a blissed-out moron. He needed his wits about him if he was going to understand how things really worked. Not how his parents had told him things worked. Not how the school or the Church had told him they worked. How they really worked. The whole universe lay at his doorstep and he felt like all it would take to reach out and learn everything was the courage to take that first step out into a bigger world.

Hallucinogens were his drugs of choice from that point on, with a particular preference for LSD, also known as acid. His preference for acid was so strong that he would, at some point during those years, get a tattoo across his stomach demanding that acid be legalised.

While the drugs did precisely what they were meant to do, opening up his mind and letting him experience reality through a different lens, they also exacerbated many of the underlying mental health conditions that plagued Herb. The marijuana had been significant enough in affecting his moods and stability, but the hallucinogens really pushed him over the edge, driving his paranoia into overdrive and kindling hallucinations that would persist for the remainder of his life.

It was at this point that many of the beliefs that would come to shape Herb's views of the world would begin to solidify. He began to hear voices in his head that did not belong to him. Voices that would tell him to do things, often things that he very much did not want to do, but he was so confused and directionless at that point that he frequently obeyed the voices just so that he would feel some sense of purpose in his life. At this point, all of his old friends had been thoroughly alienated so there wasn't anyone around who could restrain him, even when he did things like shave his own head or put out a cigarette on the tip of his penis.

Shortly after his girlfriend broke up with him, Herb approached his older sister to ask for sex. She declined, obviously, and was too surprised to really make a sufficient display of disgust. At least that first time.

She told her parents about the incident, but after questioning Herb his mother was convinced that this was just some nasty accusation that his older sister was fabricating to try and get him into trouble. He was a good boy, innocent in mind and deed. Probably still a virgin. There was no way that he would proposition his own sister.

He approached her again, repeatedly, asking her for explicit sexual favours of varying degrees of iniquity. Each time she declined, angrily, threatening violence if he didn't stop. Each time she reported his requests to her parents, who still weren't convinced. For his part, Herb didn't understand why the sister who allegedly loved him wouldn't help him deal with his uncomfortable urges. For her part, she couldn't understand what benefit he gained from making their home so hostile to live in. Eventually, she would move out to escape from her brother's presence and his constant degrading remarks about her body and what he desired to do with it. Of course, with her parents being so conservative, the only way that she could move out was if there was a husband ready and waiting for her, so she pushed her current boyfriend into proposing and they were wed just a couple of years after Herb first started going off the rails.

Yet even these increasingly outrageous behaviours from Herb weren't enough to push his parents into taking action. They knew, without any doubt, that there was something profoundly wrong with Herb, but it wouldn't be until February of 1969 that they would finally admit to it.

It was a relatively normal day in the Mullin household, with the exception of the fact that they'd be having dinner guests that evening. Herb's older sister and her husband were coming to visit, so his mother set him to work giving the place a thorough clean up. It was something that he was relatively good at. It didn't require much thought, it was repetitive, Herb thought of it as being tantamount to meditation. All in all, it was a pretty good day for Herb from the perspective of his parents, at least until his sister and her husband arrived.

From the moment that his brother-in-law stepped in the door, something changed in Herb. He was talking to everyone just like normal, outwardly behaving like he normally did in polite company, but there was something odd about the way that he was moving. It wouldn't be until dinner time that his father would finally identify what it was that was making everyone so uncomfortable. Herb's body language was perfectly reflecting his brother-in-law's. Every movement that the other man-made was being copied by Herb, not in mockery, but simultaneously. It was almost supernatural to observe. All of the other man's mannerisms. The way he dabbed his lips with the napkin after drinking. The way he flexed his fingers on the tabletop. All of the tiny little movements that were unique to him, were no longer unique.

Everyone was disquieted by his behaviour even if only one of them had put their finger on what was happening, but gradually, the rest of the family worked it out too. His sister thought it was just Herb being obnoxious, trying to mock the man that she'd married. Her husband didn't know what to think of the whole thing, nervously laughing every time that he spotted it, only to hear that same nervous laugh passing from Herb's lips too. Herb's mother was the last to spot what was going on, and she reacted with the kind of visceral revulsion normally reserved for the discovery of a decaying carcass under the table. She leapt up and scurried away from Herb, who looked after her with confusion written on his features. At least until his own expression was wiped away to become a copy of his brother-in-law's once more. The fact that Herb's motions were so closely synchronised with the other man's scared the hell out of his mother. She thought that he might have been possessed, or brain damaged by all the drugs that he was abusing. What she didn't know was that perfect mirroring behaviour of this kind is one of the clearest indicators when a young person is suffering from schizophrenia.

When she approached her family doctor with the odd story the next day, he was quick to pick up on the oddity of behaviour, and combined with the various other bizarre little habits that Herb had picked up of late, he was finally certain enough to hazard a diagnosis. To be certain of this diagnosis, they would need to commit Herb to a mental institution for a period of observation, and then afterwards he could be medicated and made into a functioning member of society once more.

This was a massive relief to his mother, even if the doctor had been drastically overselling how effective the psycho-pharmaceuticals of the time actually were. The only problem was that she had to convince both Herb and his father that this was the correct course of action so that they could get him committed. This was more of a process than one might have expected. In the case of his father, there were a great many societal hurdles that needed to be overcome. Firstly, his father had to be convinced that mental health problems were real. Secondly, he had to be convinced that his own son was suffering from them, and finally, there was the whole problem of dealing with the potential shame and stigma that would come with the rest of the community learning that their son was 'crazy.'

Convincing Herb was another matter entirely. He did not believe for a moment that he was mentally ill. In fact, at that point in his life, he was pretty convinced that he was the only person in the world who wasn't mentally ill. Everyone else seemed to be so focused on such small petty things, matters that Herb considered to be completely unimportant when there was a whole universe full of wonders out beyond their boring suburbs. He was also more than halfway convinced that he was the only person in the world who actually had the full breadth of human emotions, given how quickly everyone else had forgotten about Dean and moved on. It had only been a few years, and he was meant to just forget about him? More importantly, Herb maintained a very healthy distrust for authority, both the authority of the medical establishment which he thought was deliberately ignoring the potential of alternative medicines, and the authority of his parents. So far as he could see, this attempt to institutionalize him had nothing to do with improving his health and everything to do with getting his parent's embarrassing little secret out of the house and out of sight. His paranoia, which had mostly faded in his teenage years when things were going well, had now escalated once more to the point that he believed his parents were involved in an active conspiracy against him. That they were colluding with some dark and mysterious forces to ensure that he was sidelined and belittled. To Herb, this seemed to be the latest in a long line of attempts by his parents to discredit him and his ideas by making him seem like he was a crazy person. He wasn't going to let them do it. He wasn't going to sign up to be treated like he was crazy when he wasn't crazy. If he was crazy, he'd know he was crazy, there would be signs. But he was not crazy, he was just more enlightened than these other people. His mind was just more open than theirs were, he was open and he was listening, and when the voice of the cosmos spoke to him, he heard it. He heard the warning. He knew that the end was nigh.

During one of his more lucid moments, Herb consented to go to a hospital, just to make his mother happy. He didn't have any big plans for the week. If he could go there, get checked out, and prove to her that he wasn't crazy then she'd finally get off his back and he could get on with the important work that he had been given. Besides, despite their disagreements about religion, she was still his mother, and he did love her. If he could do this thing and it would make her less scared and upset about the journey of spiritual enlightenment that he was on, then of course he'd do it. He affixed most of his persecution complex to his father anyway. He blamed him for letting his mother take him to church as a child, because the way that he saw it, it was his father's responsibility to recognize that his wife was being duped and to pull her out of the situation. His father had enough sense not to get pulled in himself, so why couldn't he pull her out? She was a victim of the church's brainwashing, but dear old Dad was running around without any controls clamped onto his brain, so why couldn't he recognize the lie? Why couldn't he save her and Herb from it? Because he wanted them to be broken down by the lies, he wanted their experiences in the church to melt away any resistance that they might have had, so that when the time came for him to exert control over them they'd be all the more pliable. To Herb's view, this was why whatever shadowy force operated behind the scenes of modern society allowed organized religion to exist. It created ambiguity in their minds, it made them more susceptible to believing lies if they were repeated often enough. The whole thing was a trap. A mind trap, meant to weaken their psychic defences so that they could be dominated by men like his father.

So he went to the institution, and it became almost instantly apparent to the staff that Herb was suffering from schizophrenia of some sort. The mirroring body language that he'd started involuntarily performing when confronted with his brother-in-law had continued, and it gave a very clear indication that something was going on in his head, even if the specifics would take more work to decipher.

Unfortunately for everyone involved, and everyone that would cross Herb's path in his later life, deciphering the specifics of his schizophrenia would prove impossible at this juncture because he had a very unfortunate combination of traits. He was schizophrenic, obviously, but he was also paranoid and highly intelligent. This meant that when psychiatrists attempted to analyse him, they could never be sure if the answers that he was providing were how he actually felt and experienced things, or if he was lying to them for his own gain. Some sessions seemed to be going perfectly well, with Herb looking like he was perfectly healthy on paper because he had worked out exactly what the doctors wanted to hear before they released him. On other occasions, his temper would slip as he became frustrated by their refusal to release him, and more of his actual opinions would slip out, but never the full breadth of his experiences. He always held information back, and always twisted his words, both to try and convince his doctors that he was healthy and ready to leave and to obscure his true intentions for the future. While he casually mentioned at that time that he believed that there would soon be another earthquake in California, it was delivered with the same sort of casual disinterest that most people living in that state would use when bringing it up in conversation. He never mentioned believing that he had some spiritual calling and connection with the impending earthquakes because he knew that it would set alarm bells ringing. He was definitely fixated on that subject, much like he was on a variety of other things, from Eastern spirituality to his dead friend Dean. But the doctors interpreted his interest in the possibility of another earthquake to be irrelevant to his schizophrenia. They did not realize that the voices he heard inside his head, but refused to discuss fully and openly with them, were whispering dire warnings about the fate of the world. Instead, they thought that he was just expressing a not unreasonable anxiety about the future.

And so it went, with the one week of observation stretching out into two, then three, and eventually six weeks of constant back-and-forth verbal sparring between Herb and his doctors, with both sides trying to outmanoeuvre the other to gain the upper hand. Neither side was willing to give up on their cat-and-mouse game, and neither was willing to cede any ground to the other, so they remained at a stalemate. Consequently, none of Herb's actual problems or experiences came to light, and the doctors were left unable to provide him with any medically sound explanation for why they were still holding him there against his will. The longer he remained in captivity, the more defiant he became. The more convinced he was that his initial suspicions had been correct and this whole thing was just a ploy to keep him trapped. As the doctors tried more and more shrewd methods to try and circumvent his defences, Herb refined his own answers and mannerisms to ensure that whatever boxes he was not ticking were now going to be ticked. The doctors had years of experience and the full weight of medical knowledge behind them, but when they were alone in a room with Herb, all they had to guide them was their own wits and, unfortunately, whatever trouble the young man was having with his mental state did not extend to his ability to assess and manipulate others.

After a full six weeks of trying to gather enough information to provide a diagnosis, the staff were forced to give up. Unless Herb wanted help, he was going to stymie any efforts on their part to assist him, and without a clear diagnosis, they didn't have any legal reason to hold him for longer. He was released back into the world without so much as a warning. The best that his family could get out of the medical establishment was a single hushed and off-the-record conversation with a member of the staff who had worked with him. The staff member warned them that Herb was most likely a paranoid schizophrenic, even if they couldn't gather enough evidence to prove it. Furthermore, in all likelihood, his delusions would continue to exert more and more influence over him until he became a danger to himself or others.

So Herb returned home, and the family tried to move on as if nothing had happened, and as if there wasn't a ticking timebomb in the next room along the hallway.

It was at this point that Herb's fixation on the idea of human sacrifices came to the fore. He was increasingly convinced that the voices in his head were demanding his life. He was coming to understand that while the ongoing Vietnam War had resulted in a massive amount of bloodshed, should that war ever come to an end, then new sacrifices would be required to ensure that earthquakes did not destroy California. He knew that the voices spoke to him of this for a reason, even if he did not fully understand why. As such, he began to think of himself as a sacrifice in waiting, a human sacrifice that would someday be exploited to save everyone else.

He wanted to be known. Until now all of these thoughts had been internalized – he had kept everything secret from those around him because so many were involved in the conspiracy against him. If he had shared his thoughts with his family, it would have been used as evidence to have him institutionalized permanently, locked away and closely monitored so that when the time came for his sacrifice, he would not have the opportunity to spill his blood. Whatever else he was thinking at the time, he knew that he could not have his freedom taken from him, not at any cost. Even if he had to go through life completely unknown to everyone. But still, he craved recognition, at least some brief spark of it, even if it was from someone he'd never met. So he hit on the idea of anonymity. He could write everything down and he could send it to a stranger, a name and address picked at random out of the phone book.

Thankfully the majority of what he wrote in these letters to strangers was incoherent enough that it didn't raise much alarm. He didn't delve too deeply into his beliefs about the world, beyond the usual doomsaying that wasn't entirely uncommon in chain letters of the day. He mentioned the untimely death of a friend, and how tragic and meaningless it felt. He mentioned the earthquake that had hit in 1906 and implied that another was due. But what he never mentioned in any of these letters was his plan to forestall this apocalypse. What he did do however, leading to considerable concern and discomfort from the recipients of his unwelcome pen-pal program, was sign off every one of these letters with, "A human sacrifice, Herb Mullin."

In itself, that was enough to raise the alarm for many of the recipients, who had concerns that this was some sort of suicide note sent to them by accident. They contacted their local police, who in turn reached out to those in California where Herb lived so that they could check in on the man and make sure nothing untoward had happened to him.

The police arrived at the Mullin family home in June of 1970 to demand that Herb stop writing these letters to strangers, and check whether or not he needed to be committed to an insane asylum once again. But when they knocked on the door, they began to suspect the worst. There was no reply no matter how long and hard they banged on the door, and there were several days' worth of mail piled up. They were making calls, getting a warrant together so that they could force entry and discover whether Herb had taken his own life when one of the neighbours spotted them and came ambling over to explain that there was no point shouting and banging because no matter how loud they were, the Mullin family wouldn't hear them all the way in Hawaii where they had gone to on holiday.

Relieved that there wasn't going to be a corpse in their immediate future, the officers returned to the station, and faxed the case off to Hawaii, for them to deal with.

It took quite some time before the Hawaiian police could track Herb and his family down, and by the time that they did, it was becoming increasingly apparent that away from the familiar environment of home, Herb's mental health was in a spiral. Bypassing his family, the police attempted to interview him about his letters, and when he proved to be too incoherent to explain his actions, he was taken down to the station for further assessment. A psychiatrist was brought in who quickly confirmed that the man was mentally ill, possibly going through some sort of emotional breakdown, and was liable to be a danger to himself and others until such time as this manic phase passed. Herb was taken to a mental institution in Honolulu where he would remain for the foreseeable future.

This presented a fresh problem for his family. They wanted to stay close so that they could be there for Herb, visit him when it was allowed and provide what support they could during what was going to be a trying time for him, but they lacked the funds to stay on in Hawaii in perpetuity. When their holiday came to its end, they couldn't afford to stay on in the islands and were forced by their circumstances to head home, leaving Herb behind. They would write to him regularly during this period but received no response. To Herb's mind, this was just another bitter betrayal in a long line of them. Taking him away under the pretext of giving him a break from the stresses of everyday life and then ambushing him with the police and the doctors. Getting him locked up, and then flying away to leave him on the other side of the world. For someone who already suffered delusions of persecution with regard to his parents, this tipped him over into outright enmity. The years it had taken him to rebuild his trust in them after his early childhood issues were entirely wiped away in a moment. Without parents as a tether, he completely lost touch with his sense of self. Before, he had suffered from crippling paranoia and confusion as a result of his schizophrenia, but he'd always had a sense of identity to ground him in reality, no matter how warped that sense of identity got. But if he was no longer relating to the world through the lens of being Herb Mullin, he would need a new lens.

This loss of his previous personality was more impactful to Herb than any amount of psychotic breaks and paranoid delusions. The foundations on which he had built himself were gone.

Herb actually spoke to the doctors in the new facility where he was confined. Not about anything that would actually help them to give him an accurate diagnosis, he was still far too clever for that, but about his parents. About the betrayal, and how early in his life it had happened. Discussing the blatant lies that his parents told him, about communion wafers, and the fairness of the world, and doing the right thing leading to a greater reward. Things that they had tried to make him believe were absolute truths of the world even though there was no evidence in favour of them. Without the context of affection towards him, he was left to conclude that there was some deliberate purpose to these lies. That the deceptions perpetrated on him had been intended to prime him and make him gullible and susceptible to other lies later on in life. If he worked from that assumption, that his parents were in fact working against him, in conspiracy with the others that he'd encountered who seemed intent on holding him back, then that meant that they had known from birth that he was someone important, someone who would have to be tempered and controlled lest he use his power against whatever conspiracy they were trying to protect.

From these rants and rambles, the doctors were able to identify clear signs of paranoia and sufficient evidence of schizophrenia that they believed Herb would benefit greatly from medication, but he refused outright to take it. He was already paranoid. Already convinced that he was being held against his will by some conspiracy. The idea that he might take the drugs that they handed him was beyond ridiculous, and the hospital had no right to force the drugs on him. So once again he and his doctors were at a stalemate.

As with his first stay in a hospital, eventually, the doctors had to stand down and release him. There was no other option. They couldn't hold him indefinitely without a diagnosis, he could keep thwarting their attempts to diagnose him. His family were contacted and his mother flew back out to collect him and take him home, promising the staff that if he showed any signs of getting worse, she would seek assistance locally as quickly as possible.

They barely said a word to one another all the way back to California, and once they had arrived back at the family home, Herb didn't have a thing to say to anyone else either. He went up to his room, still a shrine to his dead friend, and he packed up his scant few belongings before leaving in the dead of night once his poor parents had finally fallen into a fitful sleep.

He couldn't trust them, and he couldn't be their son any more. It was time to get out and make himself a new life.

Rebirth

Herb Mullin was a yoga instructor. Herb Mullin was a Mexican, he even wore a sombrero. Herb Mullin was an up-and-coming amateur boxer. Herb Mullin was just another hippie, wasting their damn time smoking weed all day long.

He left Santa Cruz after he attracted the attention of the police while sleeping rough. He might have been quite comfortable sleeping outside and chattering away to himself, but he was making everyone around him extremely uncomfortable, so officers rolled up to move him along, only to discover that he'd already vanished. His parents put in a missing person report not long after he left in the middle of the night, so it wasn't hard for the cops to make the connection. Even with that connection made, however, there wasn't much they could do about Herb if they couldn't lay hands on him, and while a schizophrenic runaway might have been big news in the sleepy neighbourhood where they lived, once he got out a few miles distance, he was invisible again. Just another nobody who could blend into the crowd.

In the beginning, it worked. The sense of having no distinct personality or self-made it so much easier to go unnoticed out in the world beyond the safety of home. He could just take a little step back and blend in. The boy who had been voted most likely to succeed was now a ghost of his former self, impacting nothing, being seen by nobody. The boy had grown up into a man, and that man had died when his parents betrayed him. Herb was drifting, aimless.

One small town after another became home, but Herb never stayed for long. Each time he showed up somewhere new, he made himself into somebody new too. In one town he contacted the local gym to try and establish himself as their new yoga instructor, but he couldn't provide any references or qualifications that would have made him a viable option, resulting in him moving along rapidly in search of better prospects.

In the town he walked into while dressed up as a frankly offensive stereotype of a Mexican man, he lasted only a very short while before it became apparent that he didn't speak a word of Spanish. After his rapid departure, many of the locals remained mystified as to what exactly he had been hoping to accomplish with the whole exercise. Wondering if this was some sort of circus act, or if they'd been unwitting participants in an upcoming candid camera show that they hadn't heard about.

Herb's attempts to pass himself off as a boxer went even more laughably wrong. He may have known some of the jargon from his time training with his father, but he lacked the physique, the training, or even the inclination to make something of himself in blood sports. When he walked into a gym, declaring himself to be a contender, it took a couple of punches in the ring to establish that he absolutely was not capable of the things he claimed. Another attempt to reinvent himself failed.

It wasn't enough for him to simply be a person, he had to be seen, and he had to be the centre of attention. He was the main character in his own story, and whoever he became had to reflect that. It wasn't enough to get a job, settle down and live a life. He needed his life to be important. He needed to be significant.

Whether that was because of his ongoing delusions of grandeur associated with his persecution complex, or if he simply refused to settle for a background role in the lives of others is unclear. What was clear was that Herb had none of the requirements for the roles he kept trying to take on, and he was repeatedly embarrassing himself to the degree that he felt the need to literally leave and move on to a new town. To an outside observer, the whole process would probably have been utterly hilarious, but to Herb, it was one crushing defeat after another. Ego death upon ego death as the new personas he had constructed for himself crumbled to ash. With each failed attempt to reinvent himself, he was back to being nobody from nowhere. Finally, after multiple bouts of trying to be the star of the show, it was his reputation as a dilettante of illegal pharmaceuticals and a dabbler in Eastern religions that finally secured him some sort of base of friends.

The hippies and the counterculture of the 1970s embraced individuals like Herb Mullin and provided him with everything that he'd ever dreamed of. His strangeness and his disconnection from regular society were revered like badges of honour among the hippies. They listened attentively to his rambling about impending doom and reincarnation. They took it on board and believed in it with as much surety as his mother had taken to Catholicism. Herb had always had a delusional little world inside him where he was some sort of messiah being set upon by a conspiracy of those trying to keep him from his grand potential. Within the hippie subculture, he met dozens if not hundreds of people who believed exactly the same thing about themselves, people who would happily validate his most ridiculous ideas and aggrandize him as much as he desired, so long as he was willing to do the same for them and their own delusions of grandeur.

Suddenly Herb wasn't an outsider, he was the centre of a vibrant social scene. Groups of people who hung on his every word and considered the off-hand comments that had once made him into a terror for his immediate family to be motes of great wisdom granted by the cosmos. When he spoke about the Vietnam War and the psychic toll it was taking, the blood sacrifice being made to America, they thought that he was talking figuratively, in terms of the military-industrial complex and the war hawks in Washington, rather than actually believing that blood had to be spilt to appease some living earth deity that was literally suffering because of pollution and industrialization gone wild. He wasn't just considered interesting and eloquent; he became someone who got invited to events just on the hope that he might be inclined to speak. He wouldn't involve himself directly in politics and protesting, wanting to keep a low profile so that he could go on preaching his gospel to others, but there is no question that he inspired others to go and speak truth to power, to fight for their rights and demand that the world become a better place. Ironically, Herb remained blissfully unaware that anything he was saying was being construed in that manner. So far as he was concerned, he was recruiting a generation of like-minded acolytes who would help fulfil his mission of spilling blood to sate Mother Earth, protecting them all from the earthquakes he so badly feared.

The other obvious advantage of being a part of these social circles was the copious drug use. Herb had been indulging in marijuana and LSD more or less constantly since the death of his best friend. To the average person, such drugs are relatively benign and often even beneficial. For those predisposed to schizophrenia, however, such drugs are very dangerous because of the way that their effects on brain chemistry can exacerbate the symptoms of their mental illness. There was actually a massive increase in schizophrenia during the 70s as a result of the number of people who were unknowingly predisposed to schizophrenia for genetic reasons suddenly triggering their illness as a result of experimentation with those drugs. Marijuana use can be a very pleasant experience for most people, but for those with underlying mental health issues, or simply an unfortunate chemical balance within their body, it can result in anxiety, paranoia, and depression – either independently of the positive effects, or alongside them. The latter seemed to have been the case with Herb. His anxiety, tied to his delusions of impending doom, was spiked each time he used marijuana. He attempted to self-medicate for that anxiety by using more marijuana, producing a feedback cycle that meant he was constantly escalating the amount that he was using. At the very high doses he ended up consuming, marijuana can cause a degree of psychosis – a disconnection from reality, an inability to differentiate between what is real and what is imaginary. This can, in turn, lead to long-lasting, mind-altering effects – which became a very serious problem for Herb given that his schizophrenia already made him prone to bouts of psychosis without any chemical assistance.

As for LSD, experiments were actually being conducted at about this time to determine its efficacy in deliberately causing psychosis. Such experiments were originally undertaken with the intention of their use in "brainwashing" and enhanced interrogations, primarily because the drug was effective in breaking down a sense of self and inducing a loss of any sense of reality. These were of course things that Herb was already suffering from before he began experimenting with the drug, so his unrestrained drug use effectively exacerbated his pre-existing condition. Another unfortunate consequence of the drug was the overtly dangerous behaviours that he would exhibit during those periods when he was under the drug's effects. Moreover, because of the copious amounts of LSD that Herb was consuming, it is entirely likely that he developed a condition known as Hallucinogen Persisting Perception disorder. If this were the case, Herb would have suffered ongoing distortions to his perception, even when he wasn't on the drugs, and would be subject to recurring vivid flashbacks to the more intense experiences he had during his trips.

His new friends, accustomed to people experiencing bad trips and suffering the aftereffects, entirely overlooked the schizophrenia underlying everything in Herb's life, and went on supporting him in his choices. It was precisely the environment that Herb did not need. Surrounded by people actively encouraging all of his worst traits and providing no social pressure to prevent him from acting on them. They were also an itinerant people, meaning that no matter where Herb happened to wander, he'd still have a community around him.

For a time, he lived in San Francisco, drifting from one friend's couch to the next. Hippies expected this sort of behaviour from one another, and while he often didn't even know the people he was staying with, there were a plethora of others who were ready to vouch for him as a 'cool dude' so there was no need to worry. Yet even in the free and easy world of the hippies, there was an upper limit to how long Herb could rely on the kindness of others to keep him afloat. Herb had no money and unlike the majority of his peers who could call on their parents for a cash injection as and when it was required, Herb had no such safety net, which left him completely reliant on these strangers to keep him fed, drunk, and supplied with drugs. While he may have paid them back with his worldly wisdom in the beginning, the longer that people spent in his company, the more suspicions began to creep in that the deranged things that he was saying were not symbolic or metaphorical, but things that he believed to be literally true. For obvious reasons, this became a cause for some unease as the weeks became months and he showed no signs of moving on from his 'convictions' to new issues of social justice as they arose.

Recognizing that his time with the hippies was coming to an end, and with no new prospects or ideas for reinvention this time around, Herb did what he had always done when things got hard. He ran home to his mother.

It may seem that returning home to parents who he believed were actively engaged in a conspiracy against him would be contradictory to Herb's beliefs, but it is important to note that many of Herb's deepest held convictions were contradictory. He did not have the clarity of thought to follow his beliefs through to their natural conclusions because he was mentally ill. It can be easy to look at someone suffering from a condition like schizophrenia and demonize them. It is easy to say that the ones who act out violently are undeserving of empathy because they are clearly evil people who just so happen to have schizophrenia. That a more moral person, when afflicted with schizophrenia, and going through psychotic episodes, would not commit crimes, because they would know that they were wrong, even if their perception of things was distorted. This is a profoundly unfair judgement.

Herb's mind was like a blender set to pulse constantly. All of his clear and coherent thoughts became jumbled with the things that he had read in books about reincarnation, ancient religions, and the myriad voices that he heard speaking to him at all times. Voices that were not his own, were not acting in his best interests, and often sought to do him and others harm.

So while his paranoid conspiracy theory was that his parents meant to do him psychic damage and limit him so that he couldn't ascend to become the leader that his generation needed him to be, that did not mean that the other portions of his mind, emotional and rational portions both, understood that his parents loved him deeply and would do everything that they could to help him through this dangerous and difficult time in his life, even though he had never done anything but cause them distress and confusion.

His homecoming elicited mixed reactions from his parents. His mother was overwhelmingly relieved that he was alive and well, having heard little to nothing from him in all the months of his travels, while his father, always a little more emotionally distant, didn't really know what to make of the strange figure that had come to darken his doorway. Herb had looked like a regular all-American boy before he'd gone on this journey of self-discovery and he had come back looking like one of the dirty hippies his father was convinced were the cause of the country's downfall. That wasn't the end of their troubles, of course. The boy's attitude had completely shifted too. He had a degree of assurance and self-confidence that he'd always been lacking before, but while that would normally have been cause for celebration, the fact was that it seemed more like Herb had just convinced himself more fully of all the nonsense that he'd been filling his own head with.

His bedroom was not as he had left it. The drugs and related paraphernalia had been cleaned out along with his shrine. It was back to looking like a normal person's bedroom again, if a little musty, stripped of all the things that had made it his home. Reset, so that it was almost like the painful neutrality of the rooms in the hospitals that they'd sent him to be locked away in. Anger helped, Herb had discovered. To begin with, as a student of Eastern Philosophies, he had considered anger to be a failing, a weakness, but now he knew it was simply his body's physical reaction to something unjust being done. Anger was not a failing, it was righteous. He was trying to come home, and they had taken home away from him. They had made it as vacuous and meaningless as everywhere else that he had been.

But he set the anger aside and went through the motions of being a normal person for his parents. Saying the things that they needed him to say so that they'd feel comfortable having him around, explaining that he'd travelled around for a time, staying with friends, thinking about the future, and what he wanted to do with it. Every time he'd even hinted at thinking about the future before, his mother had been delighted, so he knew that this was a good tactic to get her guard down, even if he had no more idea about his future today than he had back in Hawaii.

To make plans for the future, he would need to be able to stand steady in the present, and for Herb the present, and all of reality, was currently in flux. He had come to firmly believe in his rhetoric about his importance to the future of mankind. All the hippies who had given him support had encouraged that confidence, but now that he knew he was powerful and important, he needed the next step. He needed a push to progress down the path towards his ultimate destiny.

That was why, despite knowing there was an inherent danger in putting himself back in the power of the people that had tried to lock him away for thought crimes, he knew that he had to come home, he had to go back to where it all began so that he could set off on his greatest journey yet. If all of time was a cycle, if reincarnation was a cycle, then the return to the beginning was the pivot point for the entire journey.

So when he descended the stairs back into the living room of their bland suburban home and saw his father sitting there on the same reclining seat he had been sitting on the day before he left for good, Herb wasn't dismayed. This wasn't a step backwards, it was a new beginning. Everything was progressing. He was a different person from who he had been when he left. He had learned more about the nature of the world. He had come to see through more of the illusions that prevented mankind from achieving their potential. His mind and his soul had developed into something that put his old self to shame.

He sat himself down on the sofa, paying no attention to the endless propaganda running on the television screen and he smiled. It was a vacant smile, absent of any real emotion, but it was the mask that his parents would expect him to wear for as long as he lived under their roof. He had ample practice at it by now. He'd spent his whole childhood wearing it, giving nothing away. He sat and he smiled and he felt hope for the future.

"I'm proud of you, son."

His head whipped around and he stared at his father where he sat. Not a single hair had moved on the man's head, and there wasn't the faintest hint that he'd said a word, but Herb had heard him. He had most assuredly heard those impossible words coming out of his father. His father had never once said that he was proud of him, even when he was the top of his class, most likely to succeed, a sports star who was more popular than Jesus and Santa Claus combined. Not once had his father even implied that he was proud. So he sure as all hell wouldn't be saying it to Herb now that he'd come crawling home to lick his wounds, looking like he'd been hauled backwards through a bush on his way to their doorstep.

"What?" Herb asked him, hoping the man might repeat the words and give him some clarity on this whole bizarre situation, but all that earned him was a look of discomfort. Like he was the family dog long past its years and everybody was just waiting to see him take a dump on the carpet again.

"I didn't say anything." His father said, loud and clear.

"Right, sorry." Herb tried not to wince. "Thought I heard something."

Once more, he earned a sideways glance, that same weighing stare his father always seemed to give him these days, trying to work out what was going on in his head, trying to work out whether this latest weirdness was symptomatic of something worse, something that he could use as an excuse to have Herb locked away all over again.

"You're on the right path, son. You've expanded your mind. You're the leader this generation needs."

This time, Herb had been watching his daddy's lips like the gospel might come pouring forth from them at any moment, and he did not see them move, but he had heard his voice all the same. Saying exactly what Herb knew his father would never say.

His father was bound, he was trapped in this material life with no hope of ever breaking free. He loved Herb as much as he could love him despite these disabilities, but that love would always be limited by that restraint. He abided by the rules, the lies that governed so much of the world, and he didn't even know it. He had never fellated Herb when he was a teenager, just coming into his sexuality, and for that, Herb didn't think he'd ever be able to forgive the man. All those cock-sore nights when he'd needed somebody, anybody, to help him cross the line into ecstatic release and his father hadn't even bothered. It was disgusting. Here was an older wiser man who knew exactly what it was like to be a boy in desperate need of help, who chose night after night not to bother to help his little boy, all in the name of some imaginary man in the clouds who he thought wouldn't approve. Everyone else in the world did it for their sons, even the ones that Jesus loved most of all, Herb had heard all the stories from every molested washout from here to San Francisco and he knew that it was normal for everyone except for the people that had been tricked and trapped by the narrative of what was righteous. His father didn't even believe in the pretty white Christ his mother was obsessed with, so why hadn't he just shown him the love that he was meant to? Where was it then? Where was it now?

"I'm so proud of you, boy. I might not be able to do the things that you do, but you know I can cheer you on. You're going to save the world."

It was right there, in Herb's mind. Everything that he'd always wanted his father to say. Everything that his father wanted to say but couldn't because it would be breaking some unwritten rule. His father was telling him all of it, right now.

"I'm sorry I couldn't give you the sex you wanted, but now you're a grown man, I can give you the support you need. You can live here as long as you like, safe and sheltered from the wicked world out there. I'll take care of you the best I can until you fulfil your destiny."

Suddenly it all made sense to Herb. When he'd been with the hippies, they had been talking about what was next for the human race, the next stage in human evolution, that the greatest leaders of this generation might already have access to. There had been believers in all kinds of things, people who were immune to all diseases, people who could survive without needing to eat, but the one that seemed to be unanimous was the psychic.

Herb already considered himself to be something of a psychic, because he could just look at certain things and know information about them that nobody had ever told him, but what had struck him in his conversations with the hippies was that the 'vibes' they were always talking about, where they understood one another without the need for speech, seemed to be some sort of telepathy. A low level of telepathy, for certain, but one that the whole human race was already capable of.

"You're my son, and I've always been so proud of you. I could never tell you out loud, but now you're here again and you've opened your thoughts, I can tell you everything."

If everyone in the world was capable of projecting their thoughts, it would circumvent the rules. The rules about what could be communicated. It was against the rules to even talk about most of the stuff that Herb so desperately wanted to talk about, you could get locked away and have to fight doctors for weeks to get back out, but if you weren't saying it out loud, if you could just think it to one another, then how would whoever was monitoring you know? The telepathy that every single human being and ascended soul was capable of using was obviously being restricted by some nefarious means. Some sort of blocker that the conspiracy had to stop them from avoiding surveillance. But Herb, he was born special. He was more than a normal human. He was so powerful he could use his telepathy even through the blocker. Even though they were trying to stop him, he could still hear what everyone else was projecting. Not the surface-level bullshit that they said out loud, but their deeper thoughts, the expressions of their soul, coming out unbidden whenever he drew close. Like their thoughts were moths and he was the first light that had come around in forever. A beacon for all their secret truths. A messiah for all that had to go unsaid and unheard to avoid the conspiracy's grasp.

This was how he could make the two opposing truths of his parents exist in harmony. They weren't just the perpetrators of the conspiracy, they were its victims. They longed to be set free, just like everyone else, but they were trapped. They longed to love him like he knew they did, but they were chained up in all the rules of what life was meant to be like. Victim and victimizer all tied up in one. Bully and bullied. All powerful, but painfully weak. Human.

It took a lot of kids a long time to realize that their parents were only human and could contain multitudes in exactly the same way that they themselves did. For Herb, contending with a sense of the world entirely different from what others experienced, the process was even more complex. He had to work out not only how he related to his parents and who they were, but also how they fit into the various delusions that he had constructed to explain the world that he was experiencing.

"You know that you're the one. Chosen from before you were even born? We didn't know. We didn't have any idea what a terrible responsibility it would be to raise you. But by God, was it worth it. Just look at you now. You've unlocked your power. You've expanded your perception wide enough that you can see the big-picture problems that all the little people are totally blind to. I can't believe that I was lucky enough to raise you. I can't believe I'm lucky enough just to be sitting here with you right now."

"I love you too Dad." Herb mumbled out.

His father gave him a sideways glance, pretending he hadn't heard him, and went back to watching the TV with a scowl on his face. "I can't let anyone know I'm talking to you like this, so I'm going to act like I'm not speaking to you. You can think your thoughts back to me too, so neither of us needs to risk getting caught. Imagine what they'd do to us if they knew we could speak telepathically. We've got to keep it a secret to keep you safe until you've completed your mission here on Earth."

"Alright, Dad, whatever you say." Herb thought back at his father as hard as he could.

"Now that you've broken through to this new level, we can start talking seriously about what you plan to do. Everything you ever tried to tell me, I had to pretend I didn't understand or that I didn't believe you, but you were completely right about it all. Everything you've ever believed in has been true, and I've just been pretending it isn't so we didn't get caught."

"I understand, that makes total sense." Herb nodded along, drawing another sideways glance from his father.

"The earthquake is coming son. The big one that's going to send the whole West Coast sliding into the sea. Everyone in California is going to die. Everyone you know, everyone you love, they're all going to die in a hail of rocks and fire or flooding." His father shifted a little in his seat, trying to get comfortable, or unsettled by the terrible things that he was telling his son.

Herb almost sprung up from his seat in his excitement. "I've been saying that for years, Dad. I've been trying to warn people."

"In the ancient times, they made blood sacrifices to..." His father began to explain, but there was no need for it.

"I know! This is exactly what I've been trying to tell you all along. The war in Vietnam spilled enough blood to keep Mother Earth calm for a while, but more American blood needs to be spilled or the earthquake is going to come. We need to make a sacrifice."

His father's voice softened. There was a comfort in it now that Herb hadn't heard since he was a little boy. A softness and kindness that the words his father could speak out loud had never contained, but that he now realized had been trapped in his inner thoughts all of this time. "That's right son. You are our leader, the leader of your whole generation and the whole human race, and you need to be the one to make the hard decisions about who gets sacrificed to the earth so she doesn't quake."

Until now, Herb had been elated to finally be able to communicate clearly with someone about all his ideas and theories, not to mention that someone being his own beloved father, but the weight of his duty felt painfully heavy on his shoulders now. "Damn, Dad, that's a really tough decision to put on somebody."

They sat in silence for a moment, the nonsense playing out on the TV. Herb hadn't paid TV the slightest bit of attention since he realized it was just another tool for the media to brainwash people into following the program, but he kept his eyes pointed that way just in case there was anybody watching, trying to work out why they were there, saying nothing to one another even though they had so much to talk about.

"For anybody else it would be, if someone asked me to do it, I just straight up couldn't." His father admitted. "But you... you're special, boy. You've got the gift. That's just another reason you're so much better than me, and I love you so much. The universe sings to you, telling you what it wants to happen. You can go down a street and look at folks and because you're ascending, you'll be able to tell which one of them will make a good sacrifice. You'll know what you need to do."

Herb was the one to be knocked silent this time around. He had always known that with his awesome powers would come a terrible responsibility to use them for the greater good of all mankind, but he could never have imagined that so much would be asked of him. He hoped that his father was wrong. He hoped that there was some other way. "So you're saying that I need to go sacrifice somebody or the earthquake is going to happen?"

"I don't need to say it, because you already know." His father shifted in his seat again, making Herb's eyes dart that way before he could get them fixed back on the mind-control device's screen. It was a good thing his evolved super-mind was immune to outside influences. "You've known all along that what you need to do is make the ultimate sacrifice."

Herb had been feeling it in his guts for the longest time. Just waiting for the time to arrive that he'd need to do... that. "I need to... I need to be a human sacrifice."

"No son! No." His father's voice was almost a scream, echoing in the confines of his skull. "You need to make the sacrifice. You've got to sacrifice your innocence. You've got to find the right people, using your special powers, so that you can sacrifice them, and make sure that the world doesn't end. The universe chose you. You've got to do it, even though it is hard, and it will make you sad."

A tear pooled in Herb's eye, threatening to spill out and run down his cheek before he rubbed it away with the back of his hand. "I'd rather kill myself than hurt somebody else."

All the shouting was gone, all the fear too, all that remained in his father's voice was adoration. "I know son, because you've got a noble soul and a kindness in you that can't be matched by anyone I've ever met. But the world doesn't want the chosen one to be sacrificed to it. If you died, it would be for nothing. The earthquakes would come all the same. The only way to stop them is for you to kill."

Still, Herb felt like crying. "But Daddy, how can I just walk up to somebody I don't even know and kill them?"

"It's going to be hard, son. I know it is." His voice came almost like a sigh. "But I can try to make it easy on you. Kill me first. I'm a willing sacrifice. I know that I have hurt you over the years, and let you down, by pretending not to believe you even though you're so much smarter than me and your mother and know everything you need to know. This is a chance for me to make that right. Sacrifice me. Kill me. I want you to, boy. I want to do this for you. To make things easier for you."

Just the idea of it made Herb sick to his stomach. The thought of killing his own father was too terrible to even contemplate. Sure, he'd thought about it during the darkest hours of his deepest delusions, before he'd come to realize that his parents were victims as much as they were perpetrators of the system that kept them all down, but now that he knew his father, knew that he loved him, truly loved him like he'd always meant to have loved him, there was no way that he could go through with it. "I can't, Daddy. I won't."

His father's voice was stern and solemn. "You need to make a sacrifice, son. The world can't last much longer without one."

"I'll.... I'll make a sacrifice. I'll do it. But it isn't going to be you. I could never do that to you." He forced a smile onto his face, even though just thinking about hurting someone else brought pain to his heart. "When I fix everything and utopia comes, you are going to be marching into the big bright future right beside me."

As if Herb needed any more encouragement to save the world, his daddy said to him, "And then I can suck your dick like we both always wanted me to."

There was a time when that sort of fatherly love would have been more than enough for Herb, but he was a grown man now, with a grown man's troubles. They couldn't all be fixed by his own father performing oral sex on him. "If you want to you can! But right now I need to focus. I need to tune into the global frequency and work out what the universe wants from me. I'll find us that sacrifice, Daddy. I'll make it so that everyone lives free and safe. I promise."

His father spoke to him so softly, Herb could barely hear him for a moment like the radio connection had gotten fuzzy, like the transmitter had been over a hill, but then it all came back, booming and loud in his head. "You can do it son, I believe in you. And I love you. And your mother loves you. And everyone in the whole dang world is going to love you once they know what you have done for them. You're a hero. You're the greatest hero to ever live."

Despite all his best efforts to keep his face from giving everything away, Herb couldn't help but smile. "I'm going to do it, Dad. I promise you. Everyone is going to live and I'm going to bring harmony to the whole world."

His father grunted and let out a little gas. Never turning to look at Herb, even as he said, "I believe in your message, because your message is love, and I love you, son."

They sat together for a while, basking in the glow of mutual appreciation and love, but there was still one thought that kept eating away at Herb, even though he knew there was no need for it. "The people I've got to kill, they'll be okay, won't they?"

His father could have been cruel to him. Mocked him for lacking the courage of his convictions. Belittled him for thinking in such small terms when there were infinitely more important things going on, but that wasn't his father's true nature. If they'd been speaking out loud, maybe it would have been harsh and cruel, but in his soul, his father wasn't cruel at all. He was a kind and gentle soul, full of love and affection for his son. He would offer Herb any comfort that he could. "Of course, son. You know that we reincarnate back into a new life every time that we die. All that heaven and hell stuff that your mother says is just nonsense to keep the conspiracy from realizing we know the truth. Because if everybody knew that reincarnation was real, there would be no reason to fear dying anymore. And if they can't threaten our lives then they lose all power over us."

Herb shook his head from side to side in amazement. "That makes so much sense, Dad."

"Of course, it does son," His laughter echoed again in Herb's mind. "I learned it from you!"

Samsara

Life at home was uneven. There were the words that his parents spoke out loud and the words that they spoke into his mind, and very rarely did the two sets of them match up even a little bit. Herb was under the impression from his psychic communications that he was going to be adored and cared for in their home without any demands being made on him. That they would pay for whatever drugs he needed, feed him, clothe him, and do all the things that parents were supposed to do for their children. But of course, his parents had to maintain the cold exterior that the conspiracy demanded from them. They couldn't treat Herb with too much kindness and respect, otherwise it might cause suspicion. So within a day of him getting home, his father began asking when he was going to go and get a job, to start contributing to the household instead of just taking and taking and taking.

Herb had never even thought about his relationship with his parents as being transactional. He had assumed that they would feed him and house him because they had brought him into this world, and all evidence up until this point had suggested that this was the case, but he supposed that there was a possibility of confusion or deception at play. The implication seemed to be that it was something to do with his age. That as an adult, he was no longer entitled to the very basic care that he required. It was a strange thought that ran contrary to many of the ideological values he'd developed during his travels and time with the hippies. He supposed that this was another manifestation of the greed-obsessed world that cared more about the car you drove than the kind of heart you had inside. All the songs and talks that he'd been privy to in communes and campsites all came together in his mind. This idea that the modern world was designed to pull people apart, to destroy communities and make every individual isolated, so that they had to pay for all the things that they needed to survive as individuals so that more money could be milked out of each and every one of them. Atomization, they'd called it. Breaking down the community into little isolated atomic families, then pushing everyone in those atomic families to split off and start their own perfect little consumer units.

It had been hard for Herb, when he first spent time with the hippies to listen to what they were saying, as if it was anywhere near as important as the message he had to preach, but now he saw that it was all part of the same grand system. The same grand conspiracy. But while the hippies had assumed that it was all about capitalism and the rich man setting them against one another, Herb, who was privy to knowledge about the higher planes of existence, could see that it was all tied together. Isolating people made them vulnerable to psychic attacks, it made them unable to organize with their neighbours to deal with the problems facing the world. His mother's religion as well as his father's belief in self-sufficiency and personal excellence were all part of the same wicked plan. The whole point of teaching kids to believe the little lies, like there being some all-powerful daddy in the sky who was going to spank them if they got out of line – spank them in fire for all eternity – it was meant to make them more willing to accept the other lies. Obeying authority blindly was the right thing to do. You were constantly being observed and judged on your actions, even when it seemed like nobody was around. Fitting into society as it was, mattered more than changing the things that were wrong.

When he was a little boy, he'd felt like everyone was actively working against him, even though many of the bad things that had happened to him could just as easily have been chance, but now he could see with absolute clarity that even if they weren't willing participants in this grand conspiracy that the world called society, everyone had still been working against him. And of course, they had. To keep a system like this running you had to eliminate all potential threats. A leader rising among the normal people imbued with the power to see through all the lies and to guide others to achieve their full potential as psychic warriors for Mother Earth posed such a massive threat that they had to do everything they could to crush him down, grind him up, and make him just as unremarkable as everyone else. What blew his mind was that the conspiracy was doing this to everyone, not just special people like him. It was so intent on protecting itself, that it was taking all the perfectly normal people under its care and doing everything it could to make them weak and pliable and obedient, even though most of them would probably have gone with the flow anyway.

To the outside observer, Herb was doing nothing. He was sleeping in most mornings, spending his evenings in front of the television with his dad, helping his mother around the house a little with chores, but for the most part, he just seemed to be hanging around. He hooked up with old friends again after a while and started going out every so often, but the boy who would disappear for week-long benders seemed to have vanished. His drug use had declined to almost nothing. At some point during the telepathic communications he was having with his father, he came to realize that he had been incapable of using this particular psychic power while he was regularly smoking marijuana, so he had cut it entirely from his drug intake. All the drugs that he consumed now were hallucinogenic, ranging from the chemically created to the more naturalistic, and even those he was using more sparingly because while they might temporarily increase his psychic powers and understanding, he was back under constant observation by his parents. He didn't want to draw any undue attention to himself or upset them in such a way that they might seek to institutionalize him again. His anger about the previous stays in mental hospitals gradually abated as his understanding of his parents as human beings grew. He could now recognize that they had no basis for comparison for what he was going through, so it was no surprise that they had panicked when confronted with the sudden changes he had undergone as he emerged from his chrysalis and became the leader of all mankind. Your average parent didn't have to witness their child's psychic evolution, and Herb was more than willing to admit now that if he'd been seeing the whole thing without understanding it, he'd probably have been pretty freaked out too.

While it might have looked like nothing was happening while he was staying with his parents, nothing could have been further from the truth, because Herb was preparing himself mentally for the mission that had been passed down to him from the cosmos. Working it through in telepathic conversations with his father, who had now become his closest confidante and almost a mentor, until finally, he knew that he was ready. He was prepared to go and make the sacrifice that would save the world.

On October 13th, he took his car out on a long drive. This was not any cause for alarm for his parents, he often did this sort of thing to clear his head, and they were pretty accustomed to it. Gas was cheap, it didn't much matter, and it got him out of the house, which they were considering to be a win at that point.

There was no particular direction in mind when he rolled off down the street, he just let the road lead him where it would and tried to clear his head, just like he told his parents he was going to. He didn't talk to them out loud about anything that was happening. He knew that if he engaged with their conscious minds and outward appearances, the conspiracy that controlled them would force them to intervene. They would consider the needs of one person against the needs of the many and find in favour of the individual, just like they'd been programmed to do. He couldn't afford for there to be any interference in the mission, not now when he'd finally fine-tuned the radio of his psychic brain to guide him to where he needed to be, to who he needed to be with.

More people could have been found in the city. It would have been easy to find someone there. But that wasn't where the road took him. It took him out, out into the wilderness, winding up through the Santa Cruz hills as the sun rose to its zenith and bathed all the world in warmth and light. This too was a sign. A sign that Herb was going to where he was supposed to be. Light, like a beacon, guiding him towards salvation. Not for himself, but for all mankind. He was here to lead, to make the hard choices, to make the sacrifice that would save them all from the angry earth. He was going to do it today. He could feel it. The vibrations of the cosmos were in his bones, in his flesh, his hands were shaking in anticipation of what was to come. He had no desire to do harm, but he had an overwhelming need to do right. He would fulfil his destiny. He would save them all. He could do it now. He had learned all there was to learn, and he had mastered his own incredible powers, and following their guidance he would bring the sacrifice that would usher all mankind to peace.

He might as well have had his eyes closed for all the attention he was paying to the road, to the passing hills, to anything at all. His physical senses faded as his psychic senses drew him on, bringing him closer and closer to the place he needed to be. He could hear a voice now, like a whisper on the periphery of his perception. Like he was too far out from the radio station to get a good signal. It cut in and out. But it was the one he was looking for. There could be no question about that. He was so close now. So close to his destiny. So close to becoming the leader of his generation, as he'd been born to be. With the genius of Einstein, his past incarnation. With the wisdom of

Solomon. With all the accumulated greatness of the generations that had come before, imbued in him. Making him more than just a man. Making him the amalgamation of all the greatness of mankind combined into a single body. An avatar of human greatness.

The signal got louder. A steady stream of distant words instead of a pulse. A beckoning, calling him on into the hills. All at once, as he rounded a corner in the road it leapt from an indistinct murmur to perfect clarity.

There was a homeless man walking along the side of the road. Herb saw him, knew that he had to be the victim that he had driven out here to find and went on past him, rounding the next bend in the road before pulling over at the side and carrying out one of the many scenarios that he'd concocted in his head when he was planning for this day. He pretended that there was a problem with the car's engine. This ploy would serve two purposes, it would attract the man to come over and offer assistance while also serving as a distraction to keep the man focused on the car's engine rather than on Herb.

Luckily for Herb, Lawrence "Whitey" White was exactly the sort of good Samaritan who would walk up to a complete stranger and offer to help them with a problem. He would have done it for nothing, but Herb proposed a deal. If Whitey could get the car running again, Herb would give him a ride to wherever he was headed. The purpose was two-fold. If he found himself losing the courage of his convictions or if the car got fixed too easily then being able to drive the man to a secondary location would give him another whack at the murder.

The car was an old Chevy station wagon, one that Whitey was familiar enough with that he figured he'd be able to sort out whatever malfunction had befallen it between one bend in the road and the next. He set to work immediately, ducking his head under the hood and exploring every part of the engine. Paying no mind to the youngster who he'd offered to help, Whitey checked the oil, the battery and all the other things that might have shaken loose or caused a problem with the kind of trained hand it took years to develop. He was just standing back up to talk to Herb about the fact that there didn't seem to be a damn thing wrong when his whole world suddenly went black with an awful thump.

Herb had gone around the car, retrieving a baseball bat from the trunk and returned to knock the man out. From there, he had planned to stab Whitey in the heart, in a penny dreadful rendition of a human sacrifice, but as it turned out, any more violence was unnecessary. The amount of force required to knock a man out with a baseball bat and the amount of force required to kill a man are exactly the same, and while Whitey might have been a tough old wanderer who'd made it through more winters out in the world than anyone could have imagined, he was still only human. His skull had fractured, jagged shards of bone had been pushed into his brainstem. He was dead with one hit.

Herb's hands were shaking. The bat almost fell from his numb grasp. What had he done? This man was dead. He'd killed a man. One moment he was standing there, trying to help a stranger and now…

Now he'd helped millions. Now his sacrifice would save them all. It was all for the best. It was all part of the mission. He'd done the right thing. He'd done his father proud. It didn't matter that it hurt. It didn't matter that his stomach was turning over in absolute disgust at the sight in front of him. Nothing mattered except for doing what needed to be done. How many would have died if the earthquake had struck? How many…

They had to die to protect this strata. Small disasters to prevent grand disasters. Every fault was at risk. Every fault line. They would be reincarnated on another strata, another cycle. This was not the end. Death was not the end. Dean Richardson was not gone, he was still out there somewhere just waiting for Herb to find him again.

Nothing ever ended.

He took hold of Whitey's filthy old jacket and started to pull. There were woods set back a little from the side of the road, they'd provide a suitable grave for the man who'd given everything to the cause. This mortal form would rot and decay and feed the trees and keep the never-ending cycle of life and death and life turning.

The man was Jonah, and Herb had made of himself a great fish. He had heard his telepathic voice saying, "Pick me up and throw me over the boat. Kill me so that others will be saved."

He would regurgitate Whitey someday when the time was right. His soul would be returned to the earth, and spring anew from the mouth of the whale. It all made sense. Everything made perfect sense to Herb.

Everything except the tears and the ache in his chest. He was being a child, he was being stupid, he knew that this man wasn't dead, he knew that there was nothing to weep for. Why was his stupid body betraying him? Why was it acting like he'd done something terrible when he'd saved the world? Why wouldn't his breath come easy?

He had not fallen, he had not sinned, his soul was unstained and he would rise again in his next life, once more a leader of men, just as all his previous incarnations had been. Yet he was distraught, and he left his Jonah out there in the woods instead of burying him, despite having brought a shovel along and full intentions to do so. The fish that was the earth would not swallow him down and be sated and still, but it had tasted the innocent blood, and that was enough. Herb prayed it was enough.

Once he was back in the car, he packed up his things and tore off for home as swiftly as he could. Whatever was happening in his mind, his body was still doing its due diligence to try and keep him clear of detection. He might have justified it to himself not as a fear of capture by authorities, but rather an attempt to evade the conspiracy that hated all who saw through the veil to reality, but the actions were identical all the same. He got out of sight and put the killing out of his mind as best he could.

The very next day, Whitey's body was spotted from the road and the police were called. Little attention was paid to the death of a homeless man out in the hills. The assumption among the police was that he'd probably been hit by a car and wandered off to die, and while the forensic evidence wouldn't back that assumption up, they continued to treat the death as being of the very lowest priority. Hardly surprising, given that they had just discovered that there was a serial killer operating in Santa Cruz.

Edmund Kemper, also known as the 'Co-Ed Killer,' was operating in town at exactly the same time that Herb began to kill, though Herb would only learn about this other killer far later on during a more lucid period. All of the efforts of the press and police were focused on Kemper and his campaign of terror, letting Herb's murder slip by almost entirely unnoticed.

That was the end. His holy mission was complete. It should have been over. He had done all that his father had instructed him to do through telepathy. He had fulfilled all of his prophecies, taken theories and transformed them into practice. He had done all that was required of him by the cosmos.

Yet still he felt no relief. He had expected the worst to be over, for the constant anxiety that gnawed at his guts to ease, but in spite of his mission being fulfilled, he knew no rest.

It wasn't over. Why wasn't it over?

He went first to his oracle, his father, who had previously, in his silence, spoken volumes, communing directly with Herb's mind and conveying the next steps of his quest for salvation, but it was as though his father's mind was in tumult too. Their secret communications were garbled and confusing. Strange half-remembered snippets from the lectures he'd heard from the hippies about pollution and how it was going to destroy the world. An alternative apocalypse to the one that Herb sought to prevent. If it was true, if pollution was killing the earth, then there was no question that it would strike back. The sacrifice that he had used to calm Mother Earth would be meaningless as she struck out in its death throes. All would die, man and world alike if this secondary crisis could not be averted. And until it was stopped, he needed to keep the faults in check. Everywhere he went he could feel vibrations, not on his skin but in his mind, the pre-shock tremors of the earthquakes he knew were soon to come. He had done everything right, but something was throwing nature out of balance and making the world reject man all over again.

Was this another mission, another message? There was only one way to be sure. He needed to see for himself just how bad the pollution had gotten. How badly it would change things. The two sides of this task dovetailed together. After two short weeks of being idle, he set out to kill again.

Mary Margaret Guilfoyle was a student running late for an appointment on October 24th. She was in a rush, so when a stranger rolled up beside her in his car and gave her a smile, offering her a lift, it was all that she could do not to kiss him. All her problems were suddenly solved by one kind-hearted stranger. She clambered into the passenger side, profuse with her thanks, and he headed for the Cabrillo College where she was due. They had barely made it any distance at all before she realized that her profuse thanks were the only words being spoken in the car. After luring her in and starting to drive, the guy in the driver's seat hadn't said a word. Hadn't even looked at her. But she could see his lips moving. See sweat beading on his brow. He was holding onto the steering wheel so hard that his knuckles were turning white. "Hey man, are you okay?"

He didn't answer her, fumbling down at his side for something. "Do you need a hand? Have you got medication you need to take or..."

She caught the briefest glimpse of a flash of silver before her voice just stopped. Her breathing too. She couldn't understand what had happened. It was like she'd blinked, and now she was drowning. Like somebody had snatched all the air out of the car. She looked at him, with his arm outstretched like he was protecting her from falling forward, and as if in slow motion, she followed along the length of that arm, all the way to the knife that the stranger had in his hand. Well, part of a knife. Just the handle. The rest was missing. The missing part started right where her chest began. Right at the spot where her dress was getting wet and cold. She blinked at it in confusion, still trying to ask questions, still trying to understand what had happened. That was when he pulled the knife out. Inch by agonizing inch.

That slice of silver again, tainted red, like a bruise on the steel, like…she tried to cough, to clear her throat and breathe but it wouldn't work. Nothing seemed to work. She couldn't breathe, she couldn't speak, she couldn't move and now even her thoughts were slowing down to a terrible crawl. What had happened? Why had he…

She blinked away the encroaching darkness, rocking back in the seat, her chest was empty now, the knife was gone, blood ran down the front of her dress, she was still alive, how was she still alive? As they went over a bump, her head lolled to the side and she saw that they were all the way out of town now. She'd slept through the whole drive, but if she pretended to still be asleep, maybe Daddy would pick her up and carry her up to bed, just like he always used to when she was…

The pain shot through her again as she opened her eyes for the final time. It had cut through the blood loss and the awful darkness creeping in on her from all sides. The blue sky was above them with little whisps of cloud drifting by. It was such a beautiful day to die. The kind man, the stranger, came back into sight again with the knife in hand. He must have helped her out of the car and laid her down here in the grass. Something… something was wrong, he was unbuttoning her dress, and he was pulling it down. He wasn't meant to do that. He wasn't allowed to see… She had no strength to stop him, but she need not have worried about her dignity, his eyes passed over her bare skin with utter disinterest. There was nothing sexual about what he was doing, it was all just work to him. The knife bit into her skin again, lower than before, where her ribcage met. It dipped in too deep, and he tugged it back so that when he dragged it down the length of her stomach to gut her, he didn't puncture anything that he wanted whole.

The darkness claimed its victory. Creeping in like a thief in the night to steal what was left of her awareness. Down in that darkness, she died, completely unaware of what had happened to her or why. Unconscious at last, so that she wouldn't have to suffer through the final indignities.

The sacrifice was made. His part in holding back the end was completed yet again, but there was still more work to do. She parted around the blade like a flower coming into blossom. Layers of skin and fat slithering apart as if they'd been desperate to open up all along. Blood slicked everything, her dress, the grass, his hands, his knife, but much worse would follow. He laid down the knife and pushed his fingers into the cut. Pressing in past the elastic-sheet-feeling of her still-twitching muscle contracting around his wrist, he got a hold of something inside her, something solid but rubbery and with a bit of give to it. He pulled, yanking the organ out of the hole he'd made in her abdomen. He didn't know what it was. It was a strange, oddly shaped thing, further contorted by his crushing grasp on it. It was still attached at both ends to other organs still sealed inside her, but it was a place to start, a place to expand from.

Two rough cuts with the knife separated whatever it was from the rest of her, and immediately it began oozing. Whatever was coming out of it, it wasn't blood, it smelled bitter, wrong. Herb swiped a little up on his fingers and rubbed them together, it wasn't like blood at all, it was oily to the touch, strangely tacky when his fingers parted and wrong all the way. This wasn't what was meant to be in people. People were meant to have blood and bones and muscles and a soul, not this. This was everything he'd feared, pollution, seeping from their very bodies. So ingrained that there was no escaping it. Poison. It would taint the blood that he gave as a sacrifice. It would... no wonder it didn't feel like his mission was over. Every sacrifice he made would just be a temporary band-aid over the underlying problem. He would need to make constant offerings to keep the earthquakes at bay, and every offering that he made would be inherently tainted, another addition to the problem, he'd have to… this required further calculations. The volume of blood spilled would have to wash away the poison spilled with it.

Even as his mind rushed ahead, his hands were in motion once more, drawing out one, then another of her organs. They came so easily like they wanted to be outside of her like they were rats trying to escape a sinking ship, and every one of them showed signs of corruption, pollution that had sunk in past the skin to change the very nature of man. Was this part of the conspiracy? It wasn't enough to simply rule over the minds of humanity and make them subservient to the ridiculous rules that everyone had to obey, but they wanted to change them in body as well as mind. They couldn't touch the human spirit, but every other part of them could be twisted and corrupted and made pliable and obedient. It was an added layer to things that he'd never even considered, and now he was face to face with it.

Poison in their bodies, poison in their minds, fluoride in the water, pollution in the air, the crops and the animals, sinking into them like they were eating lead paint chips.

His study of the various parts that he pulled out of Mary went on for what might have been minutes or hours, he lost all track of things, completely fixated on seeking out further evidence of his new theory. There were so many parts that he felt certain did not belong there, whole organs that he couldn't recall existing, and even the ones that he did understand looked nothing like the drawings he'd seen in biology textbooks, it was as though this were an entirely different animal that he was dissecting from the one that he had read about back in school.

He dug and he sifted and his mind was completely entranced with the task at hand, right up until the final moment when he looked down at himself and realized that he was drenched from head to toe in blood, that there were fragments of human flesh lodged beneath his fingernails and strewn across the grass all around him. He looked down at the poor girl that he'd murdered in cold blood and she was barely recognizable as a person anymore. She looked like she'd been mauled by some wild animal, torn apart with savagery. This... this couldn't be what his purpose was. This couldn't be right.

Herb suffered his first, and probably last, crisis of faith.

For the briefest of moments, he let go of all the delusions that made it possible for him to get through his everyday life, and he saw reality for what it was. It was just a glimpse, but that glimpse was enough to shake him to the core. What if he wasn't the reincarnated saviour of all mankind? What if he didn't have psychic powers? What if all the incredible claims that he made about himself and his purpose on earth were not supported by equally incredible evidence? What if he was just a schizophrenic addict hippie who had murdered two people because he'd convinced himself that it was the right thing to do?

He abandoned the body where it lay, ran back to his car, scrubbed the worst of the blood off with a towel and then high-tailed it back home. He needed time to think all this through. He needed peace of mind, and he wasn't going to find it out here, face to face with the most terrible thing that he'd ever seen, let alone done.

Escaping Karma

Life became ever stranger in the Mullin home as he crept closer and closer to lucidity. As Herb became more and more aware of the reality of his situation, and how much the imaginary world that he'd constructed directly contradicted the evidence in front of him, he became more agitated and confused. Ironically, while he was deep in delusion, he had appeared much more sane than he had when he was fighting against it. Now that he was slowly resurfacing, he was alarming his parents constantly.

Guilt began to bite at Herb now that he had no justification for his actions. Two people were dead. By his hand. For no reason at all except for the fact that he was insane. How was he supposed to deal with that? How did he even know if what he had done was real, or just another one of the hallucinations that plagued him? It had been so long since he had been truly lucid and aware of the things going on around him, that he no longer knew how to cope with unfiltered reality. He had lost his faith in the most brutal and abrupt manner at the sight of the dead girl spread across the grass, and now he was struggling to decipher how much of what he knew as the truth was actually real and how much was simply his sickness.

Emotions that he'd thought long buried had resurfaced. Old fears, old passions, all of the things that had made him Herb Mullin before he was swallowed down whole by his mental illness came back to haunt him. He grieved for all the time he'd lost, grieved for the person that he could have been, and grieved even more for what he'd done. He could not reconcile the person that he'd become with the person he wanted to be. Casting aside the foundations of his beliefs as tainted, he ended up alone at the kitchen table in the middle of the night sobbing.

His mother heard him and came in, she made them both a cup of tea, then sat down across from him and took his hands. She didn't know what had him so upset. She didn't know why he was the way that he was. All that she knew was that she loved her son and didn't want to see him suffering. "What can I do?"

Through the tears, Herb spoke softly, "I don't know. I don't know who I am. I don't know what to do next. I don't know anything."

She gave his hands a squeeze and did the only thing that she knew to do when someone was faced with a crisis like this. "Then you need to turn to the Lord."

All of his life, his mother had been trying to get him into church, to fall in line with the dogmatic Catholic upbringing that she had in her youth, but every time it had come up, Herb had sidestepped it. He had been convinced that the Catholic church was just another tool of mental oppression, stripping people of their individuality and making them obedient. Forcing them to believe in some higher power that they were beholden to so that they'd do as they were told. But that unshakeable belief was as shaken as all of the others. Here he was, drowning without any way to save himself, was he really going to turn down the only life preserver anyone had tossed him? Maybe there was more to this religious stuff than he'd thought. He reached out for the hand being offered to him. "What should I do?"

The way that his mother told it, everything was simple. There were rules to the world, order, and the chaos he had been thrown into by his illness could be washed away if he accepted those rules and abided by them. It didn't matter what he had done in his life before he came to accept those rules, there was no statute of limitations on the soul. All that he needed to do was go to the church, make a confession, and he would be absolved of all that he had done wrong. His soul, when it left this world, would be taken up to heaven where he would live in bliss for all eternity. This world, the one that they lived in now, it wasn't important. It was temporary. Heaven was forever. He didn't need to worry so much about the state of this world, because he would leave it all behind soon, along with all mankind. This was the trial that they had to face before an eternity of happiness and calm. She put special emphasis on life being a trial for her son, suggesting that he had challenges to face in this life that others didn't but that didn't mean God didn't love him, it just meant that the victory of good over evil was going to be so much the greater when Herb finally chose righteousness.

He made a promise to his mother then and there that as soon as he had composed himself enough to leave the house, he would do exactly as she suggested. She wrapped him up in her arms and murmured prayers for his soul, and for the first time in a long time, Herb felt like maybe everything was going to be alright. That maybe this was the path he was meant to be on.

Being directionless and desperate for meaning had left him consumed with guilt and misery so maybe, if he could find something new to believe in, something real, that wasn't just the product of his own sick mind, he could leave all that behind and finally find peace and tranquillity.

On the 2nd of November 1972, he left home to go and make confession, driving around until chance led him to a church in Los Gatos. The church was quiet and empty except for Father Henri Tomei, who ushered Herb in with all of his customary warmth and kindness, listening to the boy's mumbling and rambling until he was able to discern that he wanted to make confession, even though it had been many years since his last confession or communion. Leading him to the confessional at the side of the church, Tomei let Herb in, then took his accustomed position on the other side of the latticed screen.

"Forgive me, Father, for I have sinned..."

Methodically, agonizingly, Herb tried to face up to the bad things that he had done in his life. He talked about the drugs, the confusion around the death of his best friend, the alternate paths of spirituality that he had walked, the extra-marital sex he had indulged in while living among the hippies and finally, in no unclear terms he told the priest about the murders that he had committed while he was not in full control of his mind.

In a strange way, recounting it all seemed ridiculous to Herb. In many ways, it was as traumatic as going through all of it again. There was no way that this priest of some made-up religion was going to believe him anyway. No hope that the man might understand the very real holy mission that he'd been on all along. The stress of giving his confession had caused Herb to regress back into the safety of delusion once again. It should come as no surprise that in the stark silence that followed the confession of multiple murders Herb heard Father Tomei speaking to him, not through the screen but directly into his mind.

"The work that you have done is incredibly important. It is a most holy mission that you are on to save the world from mankind. It is so important that I want to volunteer to be your next sacrifice."

A smile spread across Herb's face as he heard that. Relief washing over him. He had been right all along. Everything that he did was right because he had been chosen. "That's right, you're the chosen one, the one in your entire generation who has the power to save us from the earthquakes."

There was some distant murmur, too low for Herb to hear it, as in the real world, Father Tomei attempted to give him actual advice. All that was drowned out by the sudden return of his psychic powers, his telepathy came back full swing, deafening, all the voices of all the people in the world crying out, clamouring for him to save them. He'd have to be a monster to refuse. He'd have to be a coward to turn away from his true calling.

It often seems that his delusions entirely ruled him, that he was completely unaware of the reality of his situation while he was engrossed in the fictional world that his fractured psyche had created for itself but there was a certain practicality in his actions, even when he didn't seem to be aware of them. His delusions were telling him that he had to sacrifice this priest because of his higher calling because the priest was psychically asking him to, and because it would reaffirm his commitment to the mission after a period of lucidity, which he read as a period of doubt and faithlessness. But in practical terms, he had just confessed murder to a stranger, and now he was alone with that stranger, who would almost certainly feel some degree of obligation to warn the police or mental health professionals about what had occurred. If Herb was aware of his own actions, and making calculated moves to prevent detection and arrest, then his behaviour in the coming minutes would have been exactly the same as if he followed the directions that the myriad voices in his head were giving him.

He tore open the priest's side of the confessional and dragged him out. He beat the man, knocking him to the ground and kicking him repeatedly as the priest cried out for mercy and promised that he wouldn't break the sacred bond of confession until finally Herb drew his knife and moved in.

This was not the brutal dissection that had sent Herb into his last spiral, the purpose was not exploration or play, he acted only to cause death as rapidly as possible. The priest didn't fight, but he writhed, he squirmed, he tried to get away for as long as he had strength in him, and Herb just went on stabbing until, finally, the unfortunate man of God stopped moving, stopped breathing, and became the third sacrifice to Mother Earth.

There was less blood on him this time, which was good, he'd had to burn his blighted garments the last time to be pure of the poisonous taint of the pollution. Or to cover up the blatant evidence that he'd just murdered someone, depending upon how you view his actions. Regardless, the clean-up this time was markedly less, and Herb wandered off soon after the murder was complete.

It was another terrible crime that rocked the local community, but it was also an entirely random brutality that made no sense. The fact that Herb simply followed the directions of the voices in his head meant that he rarely chose the easiest, closest, or most rational targets. Even if he were under suspicion, it would have been incredibly unlikely to point to him as the perpetrator given the evidence available. His complete lack of any rational pattern protected him from detection. None of his crimes were connected to the others by the police.

He returned home to find his mother waiting for him, absolutely delighted that he had taken her advice. She wrapped him in a hug again, then drew back to look at him. All of the pain and confusion that had been racking his features for weeks was gone now. He was back to himself again. Stable again. She could not have been more relieved. If she had known that he had sunk down so deep into delusion that he could no longer even recognize her, then it is unlikely she would have been so pleased.

Despite his returning commitment to the cause, Herb was still uncomfortable with what he had done, and what he had discovered. His father's words and attitude towards him had changed since the latest breakdown. Discussion of self-discipline bled through from their real conversations into their psychic communique. Herb had strayed from the path, and nearly doomed all of mankind, just because he had gotten squeamish about the methods that he had to use to prevent global earthquakes from decimating everyone. Even now, he found his sympathies straying to the dead. He wanted a way to fulfil his task without having to go through with any more murders. He wanted to save the world without having to make any of the hard decisions.

Once again, his seemingly opposing desires managed to dovetail into a clear course. He had to kill if he was going to preserve the future but he no longer wanted the responsibility of seeking out targets, furthermore, he desperately wanted to make his father proud of him and gain his approval in both their psychic conversations and the physical world that the rest of us call reality.

With his father's blessing, in January of 1973, Herb put in his application to join the United States Marine Corps. From the perspective of his parents, it would provide him with purpose and direction in his life while curbing his more wayward behaviours, get him out of their house so that they could enjoy their empty nest in peace, and hopefully help him finally get his life into order. From Herb's perspective, it would allow him to kill with impunity and with government backing. Removing all responsibility from him for the lives that he took while still allowing him to kill as many as were required to keep the world satisfied. It was, in a twisted way, the perfect solution.

His application progressed. Herb, aware that he needed to become suitable material for the Marine Corps, began an exercise regime, began eating properly, and most importantly of all, quit taking drugs entirely. It was the first time in his life since he was a teenager that his system was entirely purged of hallucinogens, and it made a shocking difference to the man. He developed incredible mental clarity, he was able to conduct perfectly normal conversations with strangers and his family that gave no indication that what he was perceiving at the time bore no resemblance to the reality that they occupied. Also, his psychic powers, which had already been considerable by his own estimations, skyrocketed to the point where he was in connection with every living soul on the planet. A part of a vast network of souls that surpassed his wildest dreams. His conspiracy theories solidified at this point into a framework of belief that was firm, rather than in constant motion, to adapt to new information. In reality, he didn't have control over his own mind again and he likely never would, given the extent of his schizophrenia, but he felt like he had control again for perhaps the first time in his life. It was as though the universe was rewarding him for walking the correct path.

Then, abruptly, that door to the future was closed on him. The USMC had been delighted to entertain his application up to a point, but now they were asking for a copy of his criminal record. Herb couldn't submit it. He knew that he would be immediately disqualified from service if they saw it. While he'd had many run-ins with the law as a teenager, at this point in his life, most of his interactions with the law had been in the context of him being sent to mental institutions under their advisement. Regardless, Herb seemed to be under the impression that the criminal record somehow magically contained all the things that he had done in his life including those for which he had not been caught or convicted. His parents were confused by his refusal to submit the required documents, but he absolutely could not be convinced to sign off on anything, so his prospects for becoming a Marine came to an abrupt end.

Herb was furious. He had finally found a way out of his current situation, a solution that would have kept everyone happy, and his stupid past had come along and messed everything up for him again. He needed somebody to blame since he was the chosen one, the most virtuous of all men and could not possibly be responsible for the bad decisions that he had made in his life. He needed somewhere to direct his anger, other than towards himself. After all, whoever had done this was party to the grand conspiracy to doom all of mankind, they were a monster and agent of evil, they were... It was the drugs. Since he'd quit taking them, everything had become so much easier, they were poison, pollution, he had consumed poison and it had blunted his powers all these years, and he was firmly convinced that the worst of those poisons was marijuana. That was the drug that had started him off, heading down the path towards all the rest, and that was the drug that had suppressed his powers the most brutally. Whoever had first given him weed was the one responsible for ruining his life. Not just his life. The world. They'd doomed the world and made it so that Herb had to go back to murder again to keep the whole planet from being destroyed by earthquakes.

Jim Gianera. Jim had been a friend in high school, one of the cool kids who had always been in Herb's social circle since he too was at the top of the social ladder. He'd also been the first one to ever offer Herb drugs, an illicit puff on a joint behind the bleachers one day after class. The papers still moist from his own lips. Contamination. Poison. He'd been the agent of the conspiracy, working from inside Herb's own organization to take him down and ensure that he could never reach his full potential. The man had to pay for what he'd done, but first, he had to explain himself. He had to explain to Herb who had hired him to offer Herb drugs when he was just a kid. He had to hand over the names of his co-conspirators. Herb had been on the run from them for far too long, always on the back foot, always fleeing, but now he had a purpose to him that he'd lacked previously. If he couldn't kill enemies of his country to fulfil the blood sacrifices that he needed to make, then he would hunt down the members of the grim conspiracy that was intent on dooming all the world. He would spill their blood, no matter how corrupt it was. He would wash the world clean again in blood, just as soon as he found his enemy. Jim Gianera was his first lead, his first connection to the conspiracy that he knew without a doubt had taken direct action against him.

It was time to start hunting down his enemy.

Herb Mullin was not a hunter. He had no experience in this kind of work, and relying upon the universe to guide him to a specific person seemed to be working far less reliably than asking it to guide him to a random stranger. There were methods that could have been used to track down Jim with some degree of circumspection, but they were not methods Herb was familiar with.

He drove to the last place that he knew Jim to live, walked up the drive and knocked on the door. Kathy Francis answered. She was surprised to see Herb but was able to help him in his search. As it turned out, she had bought this house from the Gianera family. She was also a good friend of the family, and she knew exactly where Jim Gianera lived with his wife Joan because they socialized frequently. Jim had moved a little out of town, to a log cabin some distance up the same road that they were already on. Herb thanked Kathy politely and then headed off to catch up with their mutual friend, his old buddy Jim.

Up at the cabin, both Jim and his wife met Herb at the door with some degree of confusion as to why he had just appeared out of nowhere, but they were polite people. They invited him in and offered him a drink and settled down in the rec room to chat. When Herb mentioned that he just had some questions for Jim specifically, Joan politely excused herself.

This was the moment that the mask of civility dropped, at least from Herb. He demanded to know why Jim had given him his first taste of marijuana. For Jim, it hadn't been a pivotal event in his life, he could barely even remember it. He had been the point of contact for almost their entire peer group thanks to his own direct access to a drug dealer, and he explained as much to Herb. He wouldn't have given the other boy anything that he didn't ask for or didn't enjoy having. This answer did not satisfy Herb, so he asked again, more aggressively. Knowing that taking marijuana would stunt his mental growth and ruin his life, why would Jim have given it to him?

Jim had some experience with dealing with emotionally unstable people, having spent many years of his life as a dealer in illicit substances, or at least adjacent to the people dealing in them. He could recognize that something had clearly gone wrong somewhere along the line for Herb and that the man was now trying to assign blame to other people wherever he could to try and avoid taking any responsibility for his own actions. He wouldn't let him. If Herb managed to get himself all worked up and blamed everything on Jim, that just meant more trouble down the line. If someone got so convinced all their problems were due to someone else, they'd throw everything away to get revenge, and without putting too fine a point on it, Herb did have some dirt on Jim, so he met the anger with his own anger. He wasn't going to let some stupid hippie junkie come into his house and start threatening him and his family with the consequences of their own actions. He wasn't going to let Herb shift all the blame away from himself. He told him plainly, that Herb had taken the weed because he wanted it. Because he liked it. Jim never had to push anything on him, because Herb was so desperate to be anywhere else, to be anyone else. He had everything anyone could have wanted, he had it made, he was the most likely to succeed but he'd fallen from that pedestal like a shooting star, and Jim wasn't going to let himself become the crater.

It was at about this point in the conversation that Herb decided to change his tack. Instead of trying to place the blame on Jim, he started asking who had put him up to it. Nobody had, obviously, they were just teenagers acting like teenagers everywhere else, trying to get any pharmaceutical assistance that they could lay their hands on. There was nobody in the world who would have asked Jim to sell weed to his friends, nobody in the world who could have convinced him to if he'd thought it would do them any harm. Besides, all of this happened so long ago, the idea that it could still be causing Herb any sort of repercussions was just crazy talk.

Herb pressed him. Who told him to sell weed to Herb?

The man set his jaw. Nobody told him to do anything.

It was a lie, it had to be a lie, otherwise everything that Herb knew about the world and the nature of the conspiracy against mankind, and more specifically himself as their savior, was in question. They had gotten to Jim, they had brainwashed him into thinking that Herb was his enemy, when all Herb was trying to do was save everyone. But Herb wasn't going to let him lie his way out of this. Jim was the first link in a long chain that was going to lead Herb all the way to the people behind the conspiracy. If Jim thought that a few harsh words were going to be enough to put Herb off, then he had no idea what kind of hero he was up against.

Herb pulled his gun. The plan was to use it to threaten Jim, get his confession, and get control of the situation again, but Jim took one look at the pistol in Herb's hand and he took off running.

If he got out, he'd warn them that Herb was onto them, the full weight of the conspiracy would come down on him, and he'd end up in jail or the madhouse or worse. Herb couldn't let that happen, not with the apocalypse on the horizon and him the only one who could stop it. He fired.

The shot hit Jim in the back, but somehow that wasn't enough to stop him. He stumbled as he went through the doorway, but some nigh supernatural force was still driving him on. Herb gave chase.

Out in the hall, he caught a glimpse of Joan Gianera just before Jim shoved her bodily through a door, slamming it shut and yelling at her to lock the door. Herb didn't understand it, the man had a chance to make a run for it, and instead, he'd gone deeper into the house. It was such a stupid move. His next shot took Jim in the stomach, and the next the chest. That final one seemed to do the trick. Three bullets were lodged inside the man, but the final one had burst through lung and heart, robbing Jim of all strength and dropping him to the ground, even as he went on shouting to his wife to lock the door.

For a moment after the thunderous sound of gunfire, there was a deep and meaningful silence. Herb could feel Jim's soul leaving his body and being drawn down into the depths of the world to sate the mother of all things living. Then his moment of meditative quiet was interrupted by Joan's hysterical sobbing from the other side of the door.

It remains unclear how lucid Herb ever became during his murders, but at that moment, if he had been thinking logically about the situation then he would have realized that he had created a witness that needed to be eliminated or he'd run the risk of detection and arrest. The specific excuse that he and his schizophrenia came up with to explain his actions later was never properly recorded, so there is no way of knowing exactly how he justified what he did next. How he justified throwing himself at the bathroom door, kicking and smashing his way through before unloading the last three bullets in his revolver into Joan's face as she huddled by the side of the bath screaming. Three bullets tore through her face, above the left eye and through her neck. There was no attempt to carry on or escape from her, no sudden burst of supernatural strength as she tried to protect her spouse. Jim was already long gone. But even as she lay there, bleeding from the head, Herb doubted the effectiveness of his gun, and drew out a knife to apply some killing blows to her still body. Three stabs to match the three bullets, and he felt certain that she was done. Victory was his once again, and another soul had been sacrificed to ensure that the earthquakes didn't trigger. Everything he had done was worthwhile so long as the world kept turning.

There was no mental arithmetic that wouldn't find in favour of Herb's actions when there was the fate of the whole world on the other side of the scales from his actions. Everything and anything could be justified.

Which brought Herb to his next problem. He could walk away from the killings here, right now, knowing that he'd done the right thing and knowing that he'd left no trace of himself that the police could use to track him down. Unfortunately, there remained a single loose and dangling thread which – if pulled – could tear apart the densely knit tapestry of his delusions and his life. Kathy Francis. She had seen his face. He had spoken to her. She knew that he was heading up here, right now, right at the moment that the coroner was going to discover that Jim and

Joan had been killed. If he was to get away with what he'd just done, then he was going to have to eliminate Kathy too.

He was surprisingly clean, given the slaughter that he'd just committed, and it took little more than a quick wipe with the towel in his car before he felt comfortable driving back down along the road to where Jim used to live. There was a poetry to killing someone here, back where it had all begun. Maybe he wouldn't be killing Jim here for the terrible crimes he'd committed against mankind, but he'd be killing someone. That made some degree of sense to Herb.

Kathy opened her door to look down the black hole at the end of Herb's pistol. She froze in absolute terror, showing none of the deranged courage that her former friend Jim had managed. The bullet took her right through the brain, and she dropped to the ground in the hallway. Herb stepped over her and kicked the door shut behind him. If her husband was home, then he'd have to eliminate that man too, just in case she had told him who the earlier visitor was and who they'd been looking for. He let that blissful silence fall once more, but all too soon he heard the distant sound of speech coming from another room. It was too high for a man, a sister or a friend maybe? He'd deal with her when he got there. He stalked as silently as he could through the house, step by careful step until he came to the closed door that concealed the owners of the voices. Two of them, distinct and... not the voices of women. He pushed the door open slowly and saw the two little boys sitting on the floor. They'd been playing together despite the gap in age. Little boys, just like he used to be. Innocents who had done nothing wrong but be born into the world. It would take a cold-blooded monster to kill them. Someone truly evil. Or someone who could justify literally any evil in the name of the greater good.

Herb wondered for a moment if innocent blood would make a more pleasing sacrifice than that of the weary and the wicked, and then the kids began to turn and look at him. If they were looking at him, he didn't know if he'd have the guts to do it, so he fired twice in rapid succession. One shot to the four-year-old's head, the other to the nine-year-old when it snapped around at the sound of gunfire. Two little boys with their brains splattered across their bedroom, across their toy cars, and the books that their mother read them at night to get them to sleep. There had been no divine guidance bringing Herb here. No mission from the almighty or convoluted story to justify his actions. These killings had been self-preservation, and no matter how Herb might try to warp things in later retellings of his slaughter, the sad fact was that there was no reason that these children had to die other than Herb's fear of being caught. Who knew if the rambling of terrified children would have even led the police to him? Who knew if their mother had even mentioned Herb's visit? If we believe that Herb Mullin was entirely consumed by his paranoid schizophrenia and acting only on the orders of the voices inside his head, then this must be the first moment where he truly did something evil, rather than simply obeying the higher authority that he had utter faith in. These children were not a sacrifice to a noble cause, they were tragic victims of a murderer covering his tracks.

Herb lived in a constant state of flux. Travelling through life, one existential crisis at a time. The traumatic events that he bore witness to, through committing them, warped his worldview, and with each new tragedy that he created, he had to deal with the psychological repercussions. His dissection of Mary Guilfoyle had given him such a crisis of faith that he briefly retreated to reality. His confession to Father Tomei had sent him careening back into the depths of delusion so that he could justify the man's slaughter and ensure the erasure of that confession. Now he had returned to his holy mission with renewed vigour, trying to hunt down the evildoers behind the conspiracy to destroy mankind, and he had been forced to do something so terrible that he could barely comprehend it. An innocent woman and her two little baby boys were dead because there was no other way for him to avoid the consequences of his actions.

Confronting the reality of what he had done would have destroyed his already fragile psyche. Facing up to the reasons why he had committed these crimes, for purely self-serving purposes, would have destroyed all the justifications that he had made to himself throughout all of the previous killings. If he were to admit that what he had done here had been murder, it would mean admitting that all of his previous crimes were murder too – the weight of that would have been far too much for the man to bear.

In a desperate bid for suitable justification for his actions, he sought a solution in the realm of his delusions and came up with one that was haphazard, at best. Drawing his knife, he moved from 9-year-old David Hughes to Daemon Francis, Kathy's child from her current marriage, only four years old at the time of his death. He looked down at those tiny broken bodies and he thrust the blade into them. He dedicated their murders as sacrifices after the fact, even though it ran entirely counter to the canon of his beliefs, which said that only willing sacrifices who contacted him telepathically should be killed to hold off the earthquakes. He had killed them. He was the leader of all mankind. Therefore, whatever actions he took for the preservation of all mankind were justified, and he had power enough to consign their souls to the waiting and hungry earth. He staggered from the room, bloodied to the elbows, and headed to their mother next. None of their deaths would be wasted. Everyone would be dedicated to the cause. He fell on her in a half-crazed frenzy, stabbing again and again until he felt like the whole world was red, then, like every crime before, he just up and left without any further effort to conceal what he had done.

There had been so much blood spilled that day. So many victims of his sacrificial dagger. He felt certain that it would be enough to hold back the apocalypse. Even if their blood was tainted with pollution, there had been such a glut of it that surely it could wash away all of mankind's sins.

He headed for home, still formulating his own irrational justifications for the very logical series of murders he had just committed to preserve his freedom. Imagining telepathic communications after the fact and amending his memories to incorporate them. Moving the goalposts of his beliefs so that his actions could still be viewed as heroic. He had given up everything for the cause, even going so far as to sacrifice innocent children when the call came. He would do anything it took to save the world. Anything.

The bodies were discovered later that day, both the Gianera and Francis households were bloodbaths, of course, and all of the murders had been committed using the same weapons within a few minutes' drive of one another. Clearly, one person had been responsible for all these crimes, but there was no reason to connect these killings with the deaths of the priest or Lawrence White. As for Mary Guilfoyle, her body hadn't even been discovered yet.

No, it was clear to the police that this sort of mass murder was gang-related, something that they considered to be confirmed once they learned that the people living in the two houses were friends and that the Gianeras had drug paraphernalia stowed away in their home. It was, in the minds of the police, clearly some sort of run-in with rival drug dealers, or possibly a betrayal on the part of the locals of some larger organized crime syndicate that was being avenged with violence. The case was passed from the murder investigators to the organized crime department, and that was where the buck stopped because nobody in that department could find any record or connection of the victims in relation to known criminal operations in the area. Even if this was less random than the previous killings, the additional victims introduced an element of chaos to the proceedings that prevented anyone from even considering digging into the ancient history of Jim Gianera. What possible reason could one of his old high school friends have had to drive out there, massacre all of those people and leave? There was no logic to it, so once again Herb escaped all notice.

With so many sacrifices committed, Herb was now prepared to take a break, to regroup, reorganize and work out the next steps that he needed to take to further his mission. The impending sense of doom had briefly loosened, but this time, the delusions had not. If anything, he sank ever deeper into his fantasy world in the coming month.

It was during that month, between January and February of 1973, that the body of Mary Guilfoyle was finally discovered and delivered to the coroner for identification. The months that she had been left out exposed to the elements had eroded many of her identifying features, but the abstract nature of the remains also made it very difficult to piece together what they were looking at. Herb had been excessively thorough in his investigation of her body for signs of pollution and corruption. Almost all of the internal organs had been removed from her body cavity, and even beyond that, Herb had surgically deboned parts of her leg to examine the effects on other parts of the anatomy. At a glance, it would have been difficult to say that what was left of the sweet girl was even human. But given time and her dental records, it was possible to connect the decaying meat that was discovered by the police with the missing girl who had vanished back in October. It was possible to provide some measure of closure to her family so that they could finally stop looking for her. What it was not possible to do was explain who could possibly have done something like this.

Edmund Kemper's murders of students in the city were occurring at a similar time, so there was an active hunt for a serial killer in action, but the level of desecration that the corpse had undergone was completely unlike anything that the police had seen up until this point. Kemper did dismember bodies to dispose of them, but it was in a methodical and sensible manner, not the erratic and bizarre way that this body had been butchered. It was such an outlier in terms of methodology that even though it was presented to those investigating Kemper's murders, they promptly rejected it as being unrelated. It was hard enough for the people to believe that there was one serial killer in their midst preying on young women who were hitchhiking, but the idea that there might be two crossed over into the preposterous.

I Am Become Death

Herb took a walk. It was February 10th, about a month since the last time that he had literally gotten away with murder, and he was feeling particularly in tune with the natural rhythms of the world. He wanted to be close to nature, to feel the good that he had done to bring things back into balance. He had taken to hiking at about the same time that he had quit all of the drugs that he consumed cold turkey, proving once again that you cannot get rid of a dangerous addiction, but only replace it with another one.

On this occasion, Herb went for his walk in the Henry Cowell Redwoods State Park north of Santa Cruz. It wasn't his first time there, as he found the woods to be particularly inspiring and helpful to his meditative practices. He departed from his family home before sunrise, fully intending to camp out under the stars with no protection but the clothes on his back. Hardly the first time that he had to sleep rough in his life, but now he was doing it not out of necessity, but out of a love for the feeling of it. There was such peace to be found in the natural places of the world, far from civilization and the conspiracies that kept it bound. He found himself longing for these places more and more as his life went on. Someday when his work was done, he supposed that he might slip away into someplace like this and live out the rest of his days in peace and harmony with Mother Nature. Far from the concrete and cars and drugs and noise and pollution.

Needless to say, the last thing that he expected to find while he was hiking through the State Park was a bunch of kids camping out illegally. There were four teenagers, three of them eighteen, one fifteen, sharing one oversized tent between them. They had left a scattering of trash all around the place and that, as much as the raucous laughter coming from the tent, drew Herb off the trail and towards them. Normally, he would have knocked on a door, but there was nowhere to knock, so he stood outside the laced-up door to their tent and coughed loudly to get their attention. One head, then another popped out of the slit in the canvas, everyone grinning up at him mockingly.

He told them that they were polluting the woods with all of their waste and that it was illegal for them to camp there. That they'd get in trouble. They mocked both of these observations roundly. Getting increasingly annoyed at these teens spoiling the natural beauty of the place, and ignoring him, Herb announced that he was a park ranger, and he would give them until morning to clear out before he arrested them. He was not wearing the uniform of a park ranger, nor did he show any signs of being one beyond his fumbled statement of demands, so they closed up their tent, and Herb could hear them continue to mock him from inside at great length.

Stalking off, he tried to go on with his hike, tried to go on communing with nature and calming himself. But like a tumour, the presence of those dirty boys in the tent slowly poisoned the rest of the forest for Herb. Everywhere that he looked, he could see the greasy thumbprint of mankind on the beauty of nature. A cigarette butt here. A candy wrapper there. Tiny and faded and buried in the mulch, but still there. Still wrong. They were ruining the forest; they were ruining the world. They were the problem, those stupid dirty boys. They were there in the back of his mind, gnawing. Their presence making what should have been perfection and peace into a discordant and miserable experience. He would not find the peace that he sought in these woods so long as they were here, mocking him, laughing, spoiling everything. The high-minded leader of his whole generation obviously wasn't so petty as to want to kill a bunch of kids just because they laughed at him, that would be ridiculous. But if they were a corruption, a poison that he had to excise to make the world well again, then of course he should. He had to. It was his duty. This wasn't some act of vengeance enacted on people, this was a purging of unclean influences. He didn't have a choice. He couldn't allow all of his hard work in making the world safe and pure fall apart because of some twinge of his conscience. He was above that. Above good and evil. He was a martyr to the cause, suffering all manner of moral turmoil as a small price to pay for ensuring the continuation of mankind.

In the dead of night, he proceeded back down the trail to where the campsite lay. Their fire still burned, pouring pollution into the sky. There were still laughs and jeers and the mindless chatter of apes from inside the tent where the boys were enclosed. All around the site cans and trash had been scattered, a testament to their degenerate nature. He would be making the world a better place without them. Even if they weren't some sickness now, they would grow to be one. They would become cogs in the machinery of the conspiracy against mankind. They would grow up to be cold and heartless men, just like his father. Men who wouldn't show their sons love, men who wrestled tiny prepubescent bodies to the ground to assert their dominance, men who'd reject the hand of friendship every time that Herb extended it. He knew no end of men like they'd become. No end of evil men corrupting everything around them because they simply didn't know that there was anything else in the world except the filth they swilled and called nectar from the gods.

Truthfully, he was doing them a favour. Sparing them from the awful fate of growing up to be men like their fathers. Sparing them from becoming more mindless and faceless automatons in the march of evil. They were still in the bloom of youth before the evil had really taken root, and he was going to sever them from the poisoned earth before it ever could.

Raising his .22 calibre pistol, he undid the toggles holding the tent shut. Inside the boys were lazing around, laughing amongst themselves and utterly surprised when a dark figure loomed up out of the night, silhouetted by the campfire. They didn't have a chance to even speak before the shooting began. One after another the bullets ripped into them. The boys in their sleeping bags doused in down. The boys still sitting up, blood splattering across the canvas. Methodically, with precision and care, Herb turned his gun on each of them in turn. Some tried to rise. Some tried to run, but it was all over before they managed to so much as get to their feet properly. If they had time to scream, it wouldn't much have mattered because there was nobody anywhere nearby that might have heard them, nobody except Herb who could only hear the steady percussion of gunshots and the chorus of voices in his head telling him that this was a righteous act, that he was making the world better, that he was fulfilling his destiny.

Self-serving as the delusion might have been, it was there nonetheless, carrying him through until he walked back out of the woods, to his car and headed off home without a single drop of blood on him. Twenty dollars and a rifle was taken from their campsite and added to his arsenal.

The bodies of the boys would not be discovered for several days, not that their discovery would have done anything to prevent what happened next.

Herb had returned home as he always did, attended his part-time job as a janitor as he always did, and carried on as if nothing was out of the ordinary, as he always did. His parents noticed nothing unusual about his behaviour, the neighbours noticed nothing unusual about his behaviour, and the randomness with which his victims were chosen meant that he was essentially invisible to the police investigation. Even if they had suspicions that he might have been violent based on his time spent in mental institutions they probably never would have interviewed him regarding the spree of random murders, and nothing in his medical records gave an indication that he was a danger to anyone but himself. He was as invisible as death itself, and gradually he became convinced that this was another of the superpowers that had been granted to him by his position as the leader of his generation. So long as he was conducting his mission, he felt sure that he was untouchable. So long as the voices of his would-be victims sang out to him, demanding to be made the next sacrifice, he felt as though he was doing no wrong and could not be judged by mortal powers.

Three days after the slaughter in the woods on February 10th, he was driving around in his station wagon collecting firewood when a voice came to him as clear as if someone was speaking from the passenger seat beside him. A new sacrifice demanding his attention.

He had thought that he'd done enough to sate the earth's bloodlust, but it seemed that another body was always needed, another unfortunate who so hated their life that they'd be willing to give it up so that the world might live on. Herb could relate, there had been many times that he wished that he could have been one of the sacrifices rather than the one having to pull the trigger. Killing was a terrible thing for anyone to have to do, especially someone as sensitive as him. His father had always said that his sensitivity showed that he was weak and womanly, but Herb had come to understand in their long psychic communions that his father was jealous of his son's ability to feel so deeply and fully. That his own ability to love and find joy and sorrow were stunted thanks to his submission to the ruling paradigm. Most of all, he had acknowledged at long last how proud he was of Herb, that in spite of the terrible burden that it placed on his soft heart, he was still able to overcome his empathy and commit to the sacrifices that needed to be made.

Herb was a hero, a true hero, offering up his own heart on a platter each time that he took the life of another sacrifice. He knew in his soul that he was doing the right thing, that he was doing the only thing that he could do to save the world from the evil that consumed it, but that did not mean he could perform his duties without pain. Every killing hurt him, it hurt his heart, but he was still willing to do what needed to be done. His father's pride had swollen up so much that he felt certain that any day he'd break through the conditioning that the conspiracy had put him through, that he would throw caution to the wind and say it out loud instead of just in their psychic subconscious communications.

The voice from the passenger's seat demanding death quieted as Herb drove along, so he made a U-turn and headed back along the quiet suburban street that he'd been travelling along until he triangulated the signal. There was an old man out working in his garden, screaming out to be killed, to save the world. All that he wanted was to die so that the world might live. His saintliness surrounded him like an aura of beautiful sunlight. Herb parked the car by the curb, drew the .22 rifle that he'd borrowed from the boys in the forest, and used the hood of his car to steady his aim. He settled into a crouch like a sniper and in broad daylight, lined up his shot and pulled the trigger.

Fred Perez was a long-time resident of Santa Cruz, he was 72 years old and had lived a long and storied life, retiring from an early career as a heavyweight prize fighter to open up a fishmonger with his winnings. A killer right hook wasn't something that he could pass down to his kids, but a business was, and the fish business proved good for the Perez family, keeping them all well-fed and taken care of until the little ones were big enough to take it over. Despite his age, he was still in great health, and the garden he preened over daily was definitely a contributing factor to that. Even if he was no longer working long days in the shop, he was still active and happy, tending to his flowers and receiving an endless stream of visits from his myriad grandchildren.

The bullet struck him directly in the heart, as clean a kill shot as any sniper ever could have managed. Lethal almost instantly, and blessedly painless too. By the time that he even knew that he was hit, he was already losing consciousness. And if he had time to wonder what had happened, we will never know.

As for Herb, he popped the safety back on the rifle, stowed it away again in the trunk, climbed back into the car and drove off without a care in the world. He was invisible, after all. There was no need for him to worry about witnesses or evidence. Not anymore. Not now that his position had been so thoroughly ingrained.

One of Fred's neighbours had been out in their own garden at the same time. They had watched the car go by, make its turn and come back. Watched Herb get out, carefully line up his shot and fire. They had borne witness to everything, and then they immediately noted Herb's license plate number and called the cops.

Literally, a minute later a patrol car rolled up on Herb and had him pull over. The .22 pistol that he had used to kill the boys in the woods and his drug-dealing acquaintance was sitting on the seat beside him, but he made no motion to use it. He went through the whole process of his arrest with a strange little smile on his face, calm beyond all reason, as though he expected to wake up from this silly dream any moment now. He was taken into custody for the shooting of Fred Perez and brought to the nearest precinct station for further questioning. The killing spree that had resulted in the deaths of 13 people was finally at an end.

Herb didn't seem to have noticed. He chatted away quite casually with the patrolman that had arrested him, as though they were just taking a ride together. Still floating along in a bubble of delusion. He was untouchable, so he had nothing to fear.

The Testament

Herb was booked and arrived in an interrogation room within an hour of his latest murder, still seeming blissfully unaware that he was going to be facing any sort of repercussions for his actions. The cops didn't know what to make of him. There was clearly something fundamentally wrong with the guy, but he hadn't pulled the readily available gun on them when they caught him, so there was a great deal of confusion over whether he was actually some sort of violent offender, or if there had been some intentional obfuscation in which the actual killer dumped this brain-dead stoner into the car to take the heat for them.

Herb didn't look like anyone's idea of a murderer. And the idea that this clean-cut ex-hippie might have been responsible for a murder seemed frankly laughable. For all that the police might have loathed the hippies, they weren't exactly inclined towards violent crimes like this, and guys like Herb even less so.

Initially, they took Herb's quiet composure as compliance and believed that interviewing him about his rather bizarre actions that day was going to be easy. They were soon disabused of that notion when Herb jerked up out of his seat, demanding in an imperious tone, "Silence!"

It actually worked, stunning the interviewing detective quiet for long enough that Herb felt that he could consult with whatever voice was currently speaking to him.

Psychologically, Herb was in a very strange and vulnerable place with many internal factors working on him.

There was an innate desire on Herb's part to confess, which we had seen manifest itself in his dealings with Father Henri Tomei, but it was a desire built of many contradictions. On a purely rational level, if such a thing still existed for Herb at that point in his life, he recognized that he had been caught red-handed committing a crime, and as such he was most likely going to be going to jail regardless of what happened next. Whatever sense of self-preservation had been operating up until now, influencing his delusions to make him commit crimes in a manner that would prevent his detection, could finally fall silent. The cat was out of the bag, and the stress of maintaining secrecy had always been too much for Herb, so this interview offered an ideal outlet for that pressure.

Beyond the venting of psychological pressure, we could also view his desire to confess as being born of his Catholic upbringing and the belief that by speaking his sins he could find forgiveness for them and no longer be burdened with the tremendous guilt that he carried for having committed them. Whatever else was going on in Herb's head, there can be no denying that in those rare moments of lucidity, he felt terrible about the things that he had done.

Another factor influencing his desire to confess to all of his crimes was his ego. In his understanding of events, he was a hero who had done absolutely amazing things to save the world from its inevitable destruction, yet he had never received the slightest bit of praise or adoration for his efforts. He was the leader of his generation, a shining beacon of hope for the whole of America, but in spite of that, in his day-to-day life, he was being treated like a nobody. A nothing. Nobody knew that he was their saviour, and now for the first time, he had a real opportunity to share his victories and his message with the world.

The final, and perhaps defining factor in his choice to make a full confession to his crimes was that he was still operating under the delusion that he was above the law and untouchable. That his position and psychic powers meant that they could not actually arrest him or hold him accountable for the things that he had done.

When they asked him again why he had shot poor innocent Fred Perez in cold blood, in broad daylight, without provocation, the floodgates opened. Every thought that Herb had been holding back since he was old enough to form coherent thoughts for himself came pouring out. The earthquakes. Albert Einstein. The drugs. The pollution. The sacrifices of Vietnam. Mother Nature. The God of America. His beloved friend died too young. The psychic communication. The parental neglect. The murders. Every one of the murders. Intermingled with his ranting and raving, he confessed to all thirteen of the killings that he would eventually be convicted of, providing details about the dead that nobody else could have known except for the perpetrator, but the verifiable facts were intermingled with fragments of Eastern philosophy and the outright gibberish that he often used to justify his choices and actions.

He had been instructed to commit his crimes. This was what he came back to time and time again. But it was not the conspiracy that he kept referencing that was behind his murders, it was the complete opposite, in fact, those trying to break free from the control of the conspiracy. It was becoming increasingly apparent to Herb that such individuals encompassed the entirety of American society from the Federal Government down to the lowliest stranger on the street. What luck then that he was absolved of all guilt because each and every one of his victims had consented to being killed. Unfortunately, this assisted suicide could not be confirmed as the only one who ever heard this consent was Herb, and even he had only heard it through the telepathy that only he seemed to possess.

The cops had no idea what to make of all this. They didn't know if this guy was actually crazy, if he was in the process of manufacturing an insanity defence for himself so that there would be a long record of his deranged behaviour before he hit the court system, or if the truth lay somewhere in between.

They dutifully took down everything that Herb said to them, filed it away for later examination, and pressed on with the interrogation, now with the distinct possibility of not only closing one easy case but a dozen more that had been unbreakable until now. The ranting and raving went on for hours with Herb finally unburdening himself of everything that he'd seen and done throughout his life. Naturally, this afforded a great opportunity for the police to jot down several selected bullet points that would later be used in Herb's prosecution.

After he had made all of his incredible claims, both about the nature of reality and his own actions, the police finally felt like they were on more familiar ground when they began asking him about six other murders that had been committed in the same time period. They asked whether he had committed those too, but questioned if he would even remember if he had committed them or if his delusions might have convinced him afterwards that he'd done nothing wrong at all.

It is safe to say that Herb's schizophrenia altered his memories of events after the fact, but in the case of his murders at least, it seemed that every single one of them had been permanently burned into his memory. He denied his part in the other killings and denied any knowledge of them. They'd been huge news and played no small part in the city being labelled "Murderville, USA" but even so, Herb claimed to know nothing about them. They went on pressing him for quite some time, intent on closing off all the open cases on the books in one fell swoop, suggesting that because the methods he'd used in his killings had been so erratic – helping him to evade notice and capture – it was entirely possible that these other killings were simply a result of him adopting yet another method. One that was consistent across those other killings.

The detectives interviewing him were accustomed to tall tales, but not to epic fantasy. Their already lengthy interview was undoubtedly greatly extended as Herb went off on various tangents involving more or less every thought that had ever popped into his head. Despite Herb's willingness to babble on until he became hoarse, there were no further confessions to be had and the other killings had to go back on the board of unsolved crimes.

Those other killings that the police tried so hard to pin on Herb were actually the work of Edmund Kemper, another serial killer operating in the area at exactly the same time. Those cases would not be closed until two more murders had been added to the tally and Kemper turned himself in when it seemed inevitable that the police were never going to catch him on their own.

The interview stretched on interminably with occasional interruptions when Herb would begin chanting "Silence," causing the interviewers to bounce Herb back into a cell for a bit until such time as they felt Herb was ready to come back and start up again. All the while, the rest of the police were busy going out into the world to do their jobs and collect all the information about Herb that they could find. They found out where Herb lived in a spartan apartment he'd only just started renting a few weeks before and hadn't even really moved into yet. They found where he worked part-time as a janitor and interviewed as many people as possible to try and establish who he really was as a person. They learned about the success he'd had back in school, the fact that he was the 'most likely to succeed' and the way that he constantly impressed those around him with his sharp intellect. But they also learned that the disconnection from reality that had led to Herb's crimes was hardly a new thing and that the worst of it could be traced back to trauma in the year following high school. The full enormity of Herb's crimes still hadn't hit home with anyone, and everyone was quite happy to chat about the odd fellow. They shared funny titbits about his eccentric behaviour and about the overall impression many people who knew Herb seemed to have that since he'd come home from his travels and cleaned himself up, he was back on the straight and narrow.

In point of fact, however, nothing could have been further from the truth. In his attempts to ingratiate himself with his parents, Herb had quite intentionally changed his appearance and mannerisms to try and more closely align with his father's values, but this was simply a mask, a deception.

Eventually, the police called in a defence attorney for Herb to try and explain his rights to him and to guide him through what would follow. In turn, the attorney would reach out to the Mullin family to find out which psychiatrist was treating Herb. The attorney was horrified to learn that Herb wasn't receiving any treatment whatsoever for a condition that was so apparent even a complete stranger could tell with overwhelming certainty that the world Herb lived in and the one that everyone else inhabited were two entirely different places.

Herb wasn't just sick the way that most people with mental health problems are, he was utterly consumed by it. His psychopathy had been brewing, completely unchecked given his refusal to accept any treatment, for his entire life. His life experiences, twisted in his compromised mind, had fuelled his delusions and paranoia for too many years. There was so little of the original person left that removing all of the sickness, even if that were possible, likely would have meant there was nothing left but an empty shell. He had been so far gone for so long, that there was nobody inside of Herb left to save.

His car was examined during his interview, the guns and knives he'd used in his various killings were found secreted about the vehicle along with a note that read:

"Let it be known to the nations of earth and the people that inhabit it, this document carries more power than any other written before. Such a tragedy as what has happened should not have happened and because of this action which I take of my own free will I am making it possible to occur again. For while I can be here I must guide and protect my dynasty."

The police had no clue what to make of that.

So Herb was moved to a cell in the jail to await trial and, while waiting, underwent a medical examination by a doctor to ensure that he wasn't bringing anything contagious into the building.

Beneath the clean-cut haircut and middle-class clothes, Herb's body was something completely different. Throughout his interviews, Herb had repeatedly claimed to hate hippies and all that they stood for. He considered them moral cowards for their anti-war and anti-violence stances. People too weak to do what was necessary to ensure the brighter future that they wanted for the world. In odd contradiction to his supposed disgust with hippies, the strange tattoos on his body were undoubtedly the work of that exact subculture. Across his stomach, the words "Legalize Acid" were inked. Elsewhere on his torso could be found "Eagle Eyes Marijuana." On his arms and legs, the text became even more bizarre and erratic. "Birth," read one tattoo. "Kriya Yoga" another. "Mahashamadhi" was the largest tattoo, referring to the state that a yoga practitioner enters when they believe that they leave their body behind and explore the astral plane as a spirit. It is a title reserved only for those who are thought to have achieved enlightenment, very rarely dispensed, and almost certainly not earned by a man who had only briefly dabbled in yogi practices during his endless periods of reinvention.

The dead boys in the woods were finally discovered by following Herb's directions. In some ways, they resembled younger versions of Herb himself. Young hippies, out for a good time. It was almost as if he was trying to kill his past self.

The whole world looked on in horror and disbelief as the facts of the case slowly but surely came to light. There was no question of whether he had committed the murders that he'd laid claim to, and his publicly appointed defence attorney, Jim Jackson, didn't even pretend otherwise. The question that was being put before the court was not whether Herb had committed the gruesome acts of violence that he was accused of, but whether or not he could be held responsible for those acts. As the police had predicted, an insanity plea was soon forthcoming.

Doctors were brought in to examine Herb. Their unanimous opinion was that he was suffering from Paranoid Schizophrenia and likely had been for his entire adult life. Dr. David Marlowe from the University of California at Santa Cruz was his primary psychiatrist at the time, and he took as long as was required to compose a comprehensive picture of Herb's mental landscape and all of the specific delusions that he laboured under that had shaped him into the kind of person that could kill so many people without mercy.

The trial for ten murders was set for July 30th, 1973. The Santa Cruz County District Attorney's Office hadn't yet assembled the full case involving Father Tomei and the psychotic break that Herb had suffered in the midst of his meeting with the priest could potentially throw their arguments about his sanity into doubt, so it was decided to address that case separately.

Herb emerged into the courtroom looking dishevelled and confused, carrying a twin-volume legal book like it was a talisman. He announced that he was pleading guilty to all charges and required no legal counsel.

This prompted considerable argument from the court. It was considered by some that Herb was not in his right mind, and that should he be allowed to proceed through the trial with no legal counsel, any resulting verdict had the potential to be overthrown by a higher court. The judge insisted that Herb receive counsel, whether he wanted it or not, leading to a shouting match. "You gave me two choices, and I chose!"

The argument pressed on until Herb pointed to James Jackson, who had been assigned to him and made a personal attack. "I don't care to be represented by a longhair."

Herb had completely turned against the counterculture by this point in his life, believing that hippies were as guilty as every other part of society for the conspiracy and confusion he'd always experienced. They had pushed drugs on him after all, mangling his mind and stunting his psychic powers. Jackson's hair was ever so slightly longer than his collar, but in the interest of seeing justice served, he did mention that he'd be willing to go out and get a trim if it would settle the matter.

For obvious reasons, there was no question as to whether or not Herb had committed the crimes for which he was standing trial. He had admitted to them in gratuitous detail, providing detailed information to the investigation that had been withheld from the general public. Additionally, he was in possession of the murder weapons and had been witnessed killing the last of his victims in broad daylight. He had definitely killed everyone that he was charged with killing. But the legal question being laid out before the court was not whether he had actually committed the murders, but whether he was mentally competent to stand trial for them. If, as his public defender insisted, Herb was ruled entirely by his delusions, and they had led him to kill through no fault of his own, then he could not be charged as a deliberate murderer. Quite the contrary, he was not in control of his faculties at the time, so responsibility would have to be laid elsewhere.

The definition under US law for legal sanity is that the accused understands the nature and quality of their actions and that they can differentiate between right and wrong. It is, by its nature, a very broad definition meant to encompass as many people as possible within it, allowing as few people as possible to make use of it as a legal defence. In the case of Herb Mullin, it is obvious that his mental health issues were the defining factor in the choices that he made, but even when his entire personality was ruled by schizophrenia, it seems that he could not clear the "insanity" bar.

The entirety of Dr Marlowe's research was laid before the court but was considered by the jury to be insufficient evidence of insanity by the legal definition. All of the interviews, all of the examinations, all of the questions that had answers that could not possibly have been manipulated. Even so, it was not enough.

In his own words, Herb had spoken about the horror and disgust that he felt over the killings, meaning that he was still capable of differentiating right from wrong. If he knew that his actions were wrong, and he still chose to commit them, then his mental illness did not prevent him from making moral choices. The idea that Herb's mental state was in constant flux, resulting in more lucid periods when he felt guilt, and less lucid periods when he felt entirely justified in his actions did not seem to be understood by the jury. They were convinced that just because the man could differentiate between right and wrong on a good day, he qualified as sane enough to stand trial.

Just because he was under the influence of paranoid schizophrenia, the court did not necessarily feel that it governed his actions. There were a great many things that Herb did which could be viewed with suspicion if you believed that his mental illness was a fabrication.

The only "evidence" of Herb's insanity was his own statements on the matter. Given how easily he had manipulated mental health professionals in the past, there was some question of whether this highly intelligent killer was simply working the system to his own advantage. A point that was leapt on by the prosecutor, who was quick to point out that several of the murders were obviously premeditated and that Herb's actions more closely resembled those of a career criminal working to avoid detection after committing the crimes than those of some wandering lunatic with no awareness of the realities of the murders.

Herb may have been trusting in the voices to guide him, but those voices guided him through anti-forensic measures of some degree of cunning, not to mention the manner in which he avoided police detection by changing methods and behaviours constantly. If he were truly just 'reactive' to his schizophrenia, then surely his reactions would have been more consistent. When the red light flashed on in his brain that said "kill," wouldn't he simply have grabbed the convenient weapon from right beside him and pulled the trigger rather than switching from knife to pistol to rifle?

There was no real understanding of mental illness at this point in American history, and with a condition as complex and all-encompassing as affected Herb Mullin, it is difficult even for people who are educated in the subject to understand the full effects. Every single psychiatrist that he had been assessed by had been stymied by him prior to his arrest, and now, with him finally being honest and open in an attempt to avoid punishment for his crimes, it was difficult for the jurors to see this as anything other than self-serving.

So despite all of the evidence being in Herb's favour, he was judged to be fully competent to stand trial for his crimes. At this point, the case became something else entirely. It evolved into a back-and-forth negotiation between the prosecution and the defence as to which charges would be accepted, and which would provoke some sort of pushback.

In American law, there is a distinction between First- and Second-Degree Murder. Second-degree murders are those in which the perpetrator intended to do harm and kill in the moment, while first-degree murders are those in which there is a degree of premeditation and planning involved beforehand. Thus criminals who expressly set out to murder others are punished more heavily than those who might have inadvertently been drawn into a situation in which they chose to kill. The defence's argument was that Herb's murders were all in the second degree. He had not even known that most of the people that he killed existed before meeting them, so how could his killings have been premeditated? It made no sense. The argument was then made that they were premeditated in the sense that he went out on the day of each crime with the intent to kill someone, but this did not prove specific enough for the distinction of a first-degree murder, which was intended as a punishment for crimes of malice rather than crimes of passion. After a great deal of back and forth, eight of the ten charges were argued down to second-degree murder and an agreement was reached regarding those cases, but two still remained outstanding and had to be settled by the jury. There was no question that Herb had killed everyone being discussed in the trial, but once again the court was asked to decide whether he did so with foresight and planning, or if it was as random as it seemed.

The subject of the day became "diminished capacity." It had to be decided whether Herb was just as guilty of killing people while suffering from his mental illness as if he had done the same awful things under the influence of nothing at all. This became the sticking point, the bone of contention that Herb's lawyer would use to keep all the first-degree charges at bay. The evidence that he used was not simply the interviews that Herb had conducted with his psychiatrists which had already proven to be untrustworthy in the eyes of the jurors; instead, Jackson presented the evidence that had been manufactured since Herb's arrest that he didn't even suspect anyone in the courtroom would know anything about. In his jail cell, Herb had little in the way of entertainment, but he had been offered paper and writing utensils, and with these, he had begun to jot out little rambles about his personal philosophy and beliefs. It is from these that we have learned so much about Herb's inner life and the delusions that he laboured under, and they can be trusted to be accurate depictions rather than attempts at manipulation because Herb never intended for anyone to ever see them. Herb meant to destroy them once his conviction was handed down and he was due to be transferred to prison.

Entering these bizarre scribbled verses into the public record allowed the jurors to get a real glimpse of the man that they were convicting, a man who was convinced that his actions were justified because he was saving the world. A man who believed he was the reincarnation of Albert Einstein, sent back to earth to protect everyone from the nuclear age that he'd fathered. A man who firmly believed that the earth beneath their feet had to be sated with blood or they would all have died. It was all nonsensical, rambling and confusing, but little by little it made the jurors understand the kind of mind that was behind these crimes. One that was not thinking clearly, to say the least.

Psychiatrist Donald Lunde also came to court to testify on Herb's capacity, but rather than expressing himself through words, he instead played a tape recording of one of his sessions with Herb in which the man outlined his philosophy and thought processes.

> "You see, the thing is, people get together, say, in the White House. People like to sing the die song, you know, people like to sing the die song. If I am president of my class when I graduate from high school, I can tell two, possibly three young male Homo Sapiens to die. I can sing that song to them and they'll have to kill themselves or be killed -- an automobile accident, a knifing, a gunshot wound. You ask me why this is? And I say, well, they have to do that in order to protect the ground from an earthquake, because all of the other people in the community had been dying all year long, and my class, we have to chip in so to speak to the darkness, we have to die also.

And people would rather sing the die song than murder."

The aforementioned 'Die Song' appeared in many of Herb's other notes. His belief that psychic commands to kill and commit suicide were being transferred to individuals around the world at the behest of some shadowy conspiracy to ensure that the human race held off the great natural disasters of hurricanes, earthquakes, and floods through regular sacrifices.

"I believe man has believed in reincarnation for maybe, consciously, verbally, for ten thousand years. And so they instituted this law… they used to do it back then, ten thousand years ago… Well, they let a guy go kill-crazy, you know, he'd go kill-crazy maybe twenty or thirty people. Then they'd lynch him, you know, or they'd have another kill-crazy person kill him. Because they don't want him to get too powerful in the next life, you know…"

The rambling on the tape trailed off, as Herb was prone to when the train of his thoughts derailed. Then he'd be left sitting as he was now, rocking back and forth, nodding in agreement with the echoes of his own words. The two people that the jury were offered as victims of first-degree murder were Jim Gianera and Kathy Francis. These were the people that Herb had set out to find and kill, either intentionally for revenge or incidentally to cover up his crimes. The jury went into deliberation for fourteen hours, trying to decide which charges should stick and which should be lessened – there was always the option of charging some of the second-degree murders as lesser crimes also – depending on the whims of the jurors. On August 19th, 1973, the jury returned, and Herb Mullin was found guilty of all ten murders, eight in the second degree, and the murders of Jim and Kathy in the first.

He was 26 years old at the time of his conviction and would remain in prison for the rest of his natural life.

On December 11th, just a few months after the conclusion of the first trial, Herb was back in court to defend himself against the charge of murdering Father Henri Tomei. Originally he entered a plea of not guilty by reason of insanity, but this was changed before the court had really commenced to a guilty plea on the charge of second-degree murder. This spared everyone involved a great deal of hard work and made very little difference to Herb himself. They could heap a dozen more convictions on him without making any change to his life. He was in prison forever.

After the End

Herb was imprisoned in Mule Creek State Prison in Ione, California. It was only there that the full details of his life story began to come out. He received medical attention for his paranoid schizophrenia for the first time. He was given medication which brought many of the more extreme symptoms that had plagued his entire adult life under control. For the first time ever, he was clearheaded enough to fashion all of the erratic and conflicting things that he'd believed through the years into coherent statements which a wide variety of psychiatrists and psychologists were extremely happy to relay to peer-reviewed journals.

Once again, we can thank these interviewers for providing us with the insights into Herb's mind that have been scattered throughout this book, but there was no shortage of completely new statements made at this point which seemed to be conclusions that Herb had only come to following his medication. With a more logical and coherent approach, he was able to make sense of the kaleidoscope of emotions and thoughts that he'd been experiencing throughout his schizophrenia. He also began to crave freedom. Now that he was aware of the situation that his illness had placed him in, he immediately wanted out, and started working with lawyers to prepare appeals and to apply for parole at the earliest possible opportunity, in 1980.

The only trouble with his request for parole was that to be considered eligible, he would first have to take responsibility for his own actions.

On March 11th, 2008, Herb wrote:

> "As a naive, gullible, and immature undifferentiated schizophrenic, I felt that every time I got close to solving my problems, someone would come along and read my mind and sabotage my mental effort, thus keeping me naive, gullible, and immature, and therefore driving me deeper and deeper into undifferentiated schizophrenia.
>
> This is what I told to the psychiatrists and psychologists who interviewed me during the 10 months after my arrest on February 13th, 1973. Before then I did not even think about such phenomena; before then I was a non-thinking and reactive type of naive, gullible and immature, undifferentiated and paranoid schizophrenic."

He refused to take any responsibility, claiming continually to have been led astray by others and guided towards immaturity. Some of his earliest claims involved visits from his aunts and uncles, where he was convinced that they had spoken to his parents and informed them that he would become too powerful in this incarnation if he was not stunted somehow. It was for this reason, he believed, that his older sister Patricia was receiving orgasms from their father from the age of six, while he was denied them.

In the early stages of his treatment, he would continue to reference his beliefs in things like telepathy, claiming that he was being psychically stunted deliberately rather than by happenstance, but as time progressed he would come to recognize what the psychiatrists wanted to hear, and what they did not. Similarly, he would carefully watch the expressions of those around him, and attempt to modify his behaviour to fit in better. This was blatantly apparent when he was younger and had not yet managed to smooth out the wrinkles in his 'normal person' performance, and he blamed his inability to perform normality for the failure of his first attempt at receiving parole.

He became fixated on finding some sort of freedom through obedience. Just as he'd mindlessly obeyed the commands of the voices in his head when he was suffering from schizophrenia and allowing them to make all of his decisions for him, he now did the same with the psychiatrists. Absorbing the language that they used and trying to compose a new mantra for life out of it.

On March 11th, 2008, Herb wrote:

"In my daily prayer life I honestly express true sorrow and true remorse for having comitted [sic]the 13 crimes.

I am sorry and I am remorseful.

I hope that that [sic]God of America will guide, protect, and improve the 13 victims and their families and friends.

I hope that they will be reimbursed and repaid for their loss in the tragedy.

I am truthfully very, very sorry."

Once again, he fails to fully grasp the concepts that he is trying to speak about, using terms that nobody else would be familiar with intermingled with entirely inappropriate appropriate ones from other aspects of life. This "God of

America," becomes a feature in many of his writings. While Herb would eventually come to identify as Agnostic, he would still claim to uphold the moral tenets of Christianity, Judaism, Buddhism, and Hinduism simultaneously. As though he could counter any argument regarding the relativism of his morality by latching himself to as many different predetermined dogmas as possible.

Ultimately, the new-age dogma of self-improvement seemed to be the language that both he and the psychiatrists in the prison spoke most fluently.

On July 21st, 2014, Herb wrote:

> "I believe I have a positive attitude.
> I accept responsibility for the crime spree.
> I am sorrowful and remorseful for having committed the crimes.
> I am determined to live my life free of crime and criminal thinking.
> I look forward to parole and plan on being a good member of society.
> I look forward to participating in organizations that help the community exist in a healthier more worthwhile way.
> I honestly believe that I have a positive and worthwhile attitude."

This new mantra served to guide him in his daily actions, but it seemed to be extremely performative, saying what the psychologists wanted him to say without him taking any of it to heart. It became quite apparent that the same cunning mind that had allowed him to run circles around psychiatrists in his early life were still in effect now that he was imprisoned.

Having learned from the experience of his notes being read over by his lawyers and the courts to prepare his insanity plea, he was now extremely careful about everything that he put to paper. Every single word was carefully chosen to reflect well on Herb, or at least to put him in the best possible light from his perspective. Every letter he wrote, every note he made, seemed to be a pitch to a prospective parole board.

Continuing his 2014 writings:

> "Who am I? What is my purpose?
>
> I am a natural scientist. I enjoy describing and explaining the phenomena I perceive in the natural world. That means I place a lot of importance in the truth and accuracy in my descriptions and explanations.
>
> Where am I going?
>
> I am in the process of rehabilitating and reeducating myself. Over the years, since my arrest, I have sincerely healed and cleansed my mind and emotions of paranoid undifferentiated schizophrenia.
>
> Because I still believe I could and should become a free member of our U.S.A, California, society. I believe I could become involved in educating the younger generations as to how and why they should avoid living lives of crime.
>
> I take responsibility for my thoughts, my speech, and my actions. I am responsible for myself. I believe I am ready to become a law abiding, tax paying, worthwhile free citizen."

He came to recognize in his later parole hearings and evaluations that he needed to show more introspection, rather than simply claiming to have been cured of his sickness so he was now deserving of freedom. He turned the new language that he had learned inwards to try and produce an account of his crimes that let him maintain his belief in his own innocence, while also phrasing things to make it seem like he no longer believed them to be true.

> "Over the years the ideas and concepts I have used to describe and explain what happened and why, have in many ways remained the same. On the stand, at the trial, while being cross-examined, I blamed my parents and family and former friends for having deliberately kept me naive, gullible, and immature. I accused them of causing me to become a paranoid undifferentiated schizophrenic, and then causing me to commit the crime spree. I accused them of knowing when each crime took place and then doing nothing to notify the sheriff or police, during the four months that the crime spree was occurring.
> My paranoid undifferentiated schizophrenia was real. From my point of view it was not until February and March of 1983 that the disease dissipated and left my mind and body, so to speak.
> These ideas, key words, and concepts did not come to me until after my arrest and before my trial. The psychiatrists and psychologists that interviewed me after the arrest and before the trial no doubt affected my train of thought by their choice of questions.
> At the present time I am involved in trying to hire a lawyer to assist me in in getting copies of my oral testimony at the original trial. Once that is accomplished, I will hire a private

psychiatrist to do an independent psychological evaluation; one that will accurately and truthfully describe and explain what happened and why... as well as how psychologically healthy I am at the present time.

I must emphasize, I am honestly and truthfully sorry for having committed the crime spree. I show true remorse in my daily prayer life."

Each time he wrote, he hit the same talking points, all the while completely missing the point of those points. He was still acting as though he had no culpability in the crimes he committed, even decades later. He still could not accept that *he* had killed – not his illness, not the people around him psychically controlling him or socially manipulating him. Him.

This came to a head in his answers to a questionnaire that he received from the prison psychiatric staff, with his answers prepared quite obviously for the eyes of the parole board, on September 30th, 2014:

"Rehabilitation: Lifer Support Group Questions"
Who were you then and who are you now?

"From 1/1/1967 until my arrest on 2/13/1973, I was a naive, gullible, and immature, undifferentiated schizophrenic, experiencing non-verbal cognition syndrome with myself as I "missed the point" about growing up, maturing, moving away from home and parents, making a living in the world and gathering and managing my own fortune.

Now, 41 1/2 years in prison, I am a mature, competent, efficient, and effective gentleman scholar."

What do you take responsibility for? When did you take responsibility?

"I take responsibility for the crime spree. I am responsible for saying that I am truly sorrowful and remorseful for having committed the crimes.

I began taking responsibility during the spring and summer of 1973 while being given a psychological series of one-on-one examinations of conscience, ordered by the court to determine my psychological suitability to stand trial."

What has changed the most in you?

"My ability to see myself as a worthwhile, competent, efficient, and effective person living accordingly within the culture of America and California. Now I know who I am and where I am. Maturity and mental health, sanity and a feeling of self confidence, these realities are emanating from me; for this I am expressing gratitude and thanksgiving."

How have you addressed your ties?

"During my one-on-one relationships with Doctor Gordon Haiberg and Doctor Morton Felix, in 1975 and 1976, when I was 28 and 29 years old, we came to the conclusion that it would be best for my mental health rehabilitation, if I were to stop writing and visiting and associating with my parents and family. By the time I because [sic] 30 years old I had stopped visiting my former family. By the time I became 36 years old I had stopped writing my family. My life has improved because of this."

What have you done to show remorse?

"In my daily prayer life I show true sorrow and true remorse. I hope constantly that the God of America will guide, protect, and improve the victims and their families and friends. Presumably the God of America can and will reimburse them normally and naturally.

I began to feel remorse during the trial in the summer of 1973. The sorrow and remorse was complete by the summer time of 1983."

Have you accepted that you may die in prison?

"Yes, I have. Just the same, I hope I will be allowed parole soon."

What are your triggers?

"This question is referring to the susceptibility to acting out violently. My triggers are associating with inappropriate companions, alcohol abuse, marijuana, and

L.S.D. experimentation. Knowing this to be the case, I have entered into and progressed through Alcoholics Anonymous, Narcotics Anonymous, one-on-one psychotherapy, group therapy, cognitive behavior training therapy, and am presently involved in the Al-Anon Family group activities.

I believe I am in control of myself and that my triggers have been dismantled and thrown away.

Knowing that you have not had the opportunity to make personal amends with your victims or their families, what would you say if given the chance?

I would tell them that I am very sorry for having victimized them. I would express my remorse for having broken the laws of our nation, state, and country, and that they suffered because of my inappropriate and unlawful behavior. I would say that I am sorry and that I have been in California State Prison for the past 41 1/2 years trying to rehabilitate and re-educate myself, as well as trying to express true sorrow and true remorse."

How can you assure the board of parole hearings that upon your release you will live a life without violence?

"My basic belief and exhortation is that I will, upon parole from CDCR, join groups that are approved by my parole officer and his/her supervisor; groups such as Alcoholics Anonymous, Narcotics Anonymous, Al-Anon, as well as local approved religious groups. The groups and my personal sponsors will coordinate with my parole officer and his/her supervisors, to ensure that my behavior remains non-violent and law abiding."

Why should the board let you out?

"The board should realize by reading my personal written central file statements and by reading my oral testimony at my previous parole consideration hearings, and by my behavior and CDCR work records, and by my personal appearance and behavior during the forthcoming parole consideration hearing, that I am suitable and worthy of parole. 41 1/2 years within the CDCR has rehabilitated and re-educated me. I am ready and capable and worthy to be released and begin a new phase of my life as a free, tax paying, beneficial member of our U.S.A, California, society.

Once I am on parole I can contact a private psychiatrist unaffiliated with the CDCR and get a new psychological perspective on myself. This will no doubt satisfy my parole officer and his/her supervisors that I am on the right path.

The board of parole hearings has the power to make these worthwhile and beneficial activities begin to take place. I hope and pray that they choose to vote for my parole."

The parole that Herb was so desperately seeking would never be granted to him. Even if every member of the board could have been convinced that his statements were real, and not simply manipulation, the truth remained that the legal system was not solely concerned with rehabilitation, but also with retribution. Even if he was fully rehabilitated as he claimed, the fact of the matter was that he had not suffered enough punishment for the tastes of the legal system or the families of his victims. The idea that he might one day be free was unconscionable.

Yet Herb persisted. Writing incessantly about himself to anyone that would listen, trying to convince strangers to give him another chance at freedom when he had used the last chance to kill thirteen people.

> "What brought me to forgive myself?
>
> I saw that I was basically a good person who desires to give and receive beneficial blessings. Life, here in the U.S.A. and California is truly a blessing. I want to share.
>
> Have I forgiven my background and upbringing?
>
> Yes, by all means! But the ideas and concepts that brought me to even suspect their involvement, have not gone away. My former parents, aunts and uncles, sister and brother-in-law, cousins, friends, neighbours, schools, churches, etc. all in all have disappeared from my life. Whenever I meet with a parole board or psychological review board, or CDCR case worker, we always discuss the relevance and/or pertinence of those people and institutions. But my forgiveness is real and sincere.
>
> Have I forgiven the prison system?
>
> Yes! In fact it is the prison system that has assisted me in overcoming the paranoid

undifferentiated schizophrenia that actually caused the crime spree.

Have I forgiven the victims and victims' families?

Yes, by all means! I hope that the God of America will somehow reimburse them and console them for their loss. God bless America, God bless California, and God bless the victims, their families, and their friends. I am very, very sorry for having committed the series of crimes. I honestly show true sorrow and true remorse in my daily prayer life."

Because he believed the legal system to be governed by Christians, there were always references to prayer and praise in all of his writings. Just as there were references to the psychological language he had been taught albeit filtered through his own beliefs.

The psychiatrists who treated Herb seemed to be entirely convinced by his later years that he was no longer under the yoke of his schizophrenia and could have been trusted with freedom. But there was one dissenting voice regarding Herb's motivations. One person who had a unique insight into the mind of a serial killer who considered all of Herb's attempts to shunt away responsibility to a sickness to be nothing more than a smokescreen.

There were two serial killers operating in Santa Cruz California at the same time. Herb Mullin, and Edmund Kemper. To the amusement of someone in Mule Creek Prison, they were given adjoining cells.

Kemper had an immediate dislike for Mullin, believing that he had killed for no good reason. Likewise, Herb was contemptuous of Kemper, who he considered to be a sex-obsessed freak who had killed for nothing more than his own gratification, while Herb had a sacred mission.

On top of this fundamental schism between the pair, there was also the fact that Kemper found Herb to be genuinely annoying. He would sing to himself, and sometimes do so while others were trying to enjoy their limited television time. Many of the other inmates were scared of the man, so did nothing to intervene, but Kemper was a different animal entirely.

Each time that Herb sang, Kemper would spray him with water. Each time that Herb asked permission before singing, he would be rewarded with a peanut. It was the most basic of operant conditioning and it worked wonders. Despite still considering him to be the lowest of the low, Kemper afterwards considered his training of Herb Mullin to have been time well spent, as he was half convinced he could have had the man do anything for a reward. "Herbie loved peanuts."

Throughout all of this Kemper had studied Herb, analysing his behaviour, his speech, and sifting through what he considered to be affectations before arriving at the core of the man. A blackened heart exactly the same as Kemper's own. Herb had not killed because of his schizophrenia, the schizophrenia had simply been the excuse that he used to allow himself to kill. Kemper called him a "kindred spirit there," because while Herb may have made excuses to act out his hatred and rage on strangers instead of those close to him, they had both come from a similar place. A family that made them unhappy, circumstances that did not allow them to flourish despite their immense intelligence, hate and rage and pain, that they both expressed through violence against strangers. The only distinction between the two of them, in Kemper's eyes, was that he had the courage to admit that these dark forces were a part of him and not some ephemeral external force that made him commit his crimes. The devil had not made Kemper kill, Kemper was the devil.

Once, he addressed his neighbour to tell him, "Herbie, I know what happened. Don't give me that bullshit about earthquakes and don't give me that crap about God was telling you to do it. I say you couldn't even be talking to me now if God was talking to you because of the pressure I'm putting on you right now, these little shocking insights into what you did, God would start talking to you right now if you were that kind of ill. Because I grew up with people like that."

Kemper had experience with schizophrenics in his family, and had quite accurately hit upon the fact that Herb did not seem to succumb to flares of his illness in moments of psychological distress. It was a detail about schizophrenia that Herb, with no hands-on experience with the illness, would not have known about, but which Kemper immediately hit upon as evidence that Herb's "schizophrenia" was all an act meant to absolve him of his guilt. To make him more palatable to the public, and to the parole board. An insanity defence that had overrun every aspect of his life.

On August 18th, 2022, Herb Mullin died at the age of 75 while housed in the California Health Care Facility; a hospital for convicts with ongoing health issues. His death was ruled to have been by natural causes, and no further investigation was undertaken. He had been denied parole eight times, with his next opportunity to apply coming in 2025.

When discussing the case of Herb Mullin it is very easy to lay the blame entirely on schizophrenia. The voices in his head made him violent, they made him kill, they made him do all manner of terrible things while convincing him that he was actually a hero saving the world. But that is not an accurate reflection of schizophrenia. Very few people who suffer from schizophrenia are violent. With the majority of those who *are* violent, they do considerably more damage to themselves than to others. In fact, people who suffer from schizophrenia are statistically less likely to be involved in acts of violence or killing than the general population. As victims of violence, they're greatly overrepresented, but as perpetrators, the opposite is true. Schizophrenia did not make Herb Mullin into a killer.

He would claim that it made him into a victim, that it made him mentally weak and pliable so that he would obey whatever command he received, but that too proves to be entirely untrue. There were extensive studies into whether heavy LSD usage could induce schizophrenia, and whether dosing people with it and exposing them to "programming" might turn them into obedient little servants, assassins, or whatever else was required of them, and across the board the answer came back that no, it did not. The experiments went on for far longer than they should have during the Cold War, as America and Russia competed to create sleeper agents and spies out of average, everyday people, but those experiments were always a crushing failure. Some small part of Herb's paranoid delusions about society may have been proven correct by these experiments.

Regardless, the unfortunate facts of the matter remain that the most accurate psychological analysis that we've ever gotten of Herb Mullin may very well have come from the psychopath that he was imprisoned beside. Herb bears all the hallmarks of a typical serial killer, with the addition of schizophrenia being one of the few things that differentiates him from the rest. While the average serial killer – if such a thing exists – spends their time obsessing over their kills for psychosexual gratification, Herb's delusions of grandeur slipped in to take the place of such things. Instead of spending all of his time in a world of imagination devoted to fulfilling his base needs, he instead spent his time imagining himself to be a heroic savior, rescuing the wicked world from itself.

Functionally, there was no difference between the two obsessions. Both resulted in the same slaughter. The only distinction seems to be that the gratification was of Herb's ego rather than his sex drive.

It is true that there was arrested development in Herb, that he never progressed emotionally beyond his teenage years, and never became an adult in the truest sense. Instead he retreated inside himself, inside his fantasies and delusions as a way to escape from a world that he just found too difficult to deal with. But this was not a result of his parents withholding sexual gratification from him as a child, obviously. Nor was it due to some grand conspiracy to keep him from developing his psychic powers and ruling the world. He was immature because when others were putting the work in to grow and become better people, he obsessed over old slights and fantasies. Where others who suffered from schizophrenia sought help, Herb instead chose to sink deeper and deeper into his daydream world where he was the hero riding in on a shining steed to slay the dragon. The real world is a complex place, the solutions to the problems in it are not so simple as saying the magic word and stabbing the right enemy. Herb dipped into dozens of different philosophies and religions, taking whatever dressing he liked from each of them and draping them over himself to enhance his appearance as the central messiah figure in his own universe, but he never delved into any of them deeply enough to come close to anything resembling wisdom. He never put in the time and effort that it would take to enlighten himself, because if he had, he would have been forced to grow out of his self-obsession. And ultimately, more than death, destruction, and the apocalypse itself, that was what frightened Herb the most. The idea that he was not the centre of the universe. That he was not the hero of some great story. That he was, ultimately, just a rather boring and normal human being, who would have to get up every day, go to work, pay bills, and live in the world that he liked to imagine he was saving.

    Mediocrity was the curse that stalked Herb Mullin throughout his life. No matter how much he tried to aggrandise himself or numb his awareness with drugs and delusion, he died of natural causes as an old man, having achieved nothing of worth or note. He was exactly as mediocre as he'd always feared.

RYAN GREEN

Want More?

Did you enjoy *I Hear Voices* and want some more True Crime?

YOUR FREE BOOK IS WAITING

From bestselling author Ryan Green

There is a man who is officially classed as "**Britain's most dangerous prisoner**"

The man's name is Robert Maudsley, and his crimes earned him the nickname "**Hannibal the Cannibal**"

This free book is an exploration of his story…

amazonkindle nook kobo iBooks

★★★★★ *"Ryan brings the horrifying details to life. I can't wait to read more by this author!"*

Get a free copy of **Robert Maudsley: Hannibal the Cannibal** when you sign up to join my Reader's Group.

www.ryangreenbooks.com/free-book

Every Review Helps

If you enjoyed the book and have a moment to spare, I would really appreciate a short review on Amazon. Your help in spreading the word is gratefully received and reviews make a huge difference to helping new readers find me. Without reviewers, us self-published authors would have a hard time!

Type in your link below to be taken straight to my book review page.

US   geni.us/voicesUS

UK   geni.us/voicesUK

Australia   geni.us/voicesAUS

Canada   geni.us/voicesCA

Thank you! I can't wait to read your thoughts.

About Ryan Green

Ryan Green is a true crime author who lives in Herefordshire, England with his wife, three children, and two dogs. Outside of writing and spending time with his family, Ryan enjoys walking, reading and windsurfing.

Ryan is fascinated with History, Psychology and True Crime. In 2015, he finally started researching and writing his own work and at the end of the year, he released his first book on Britain's most notorious serial killer, Harold Shipman.

He has since written several books on lesser-known subjects, and taken the unique approach of writing from the killer's perspective. He narrates some of the most chilling scenes you'll encounter in the True Crime genre.

You can sign up to Ryan's newsletter to receive a free book, updates, and the latest releases at:

WWW.RYANGREENBOOKS.COM

More Books by Ryan Green

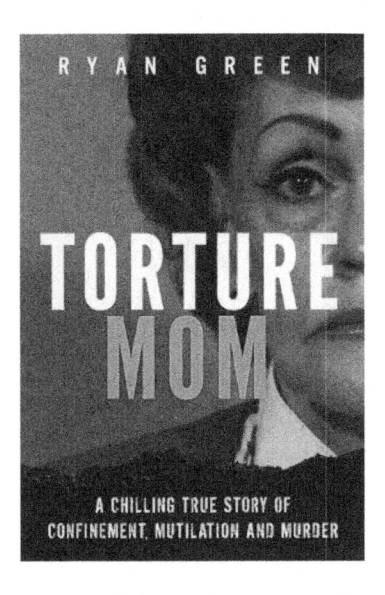

In July 1965, teenagers Sylvia and Jenny Likens were left in the temporary care of Gertrude Baniszewski, a middle-aged single mother and her seven children.

The Baniszewski household was overrun with children. There were few rules and ample freedom. Sadly, the environment created a dangerous hierarchy of social Darwinism where the strong preyed on the weak.

What transpired in the following three months was both riveting and chilling. The case shocked the entire nation and would later be described as "The single worst crime perpetuated against an individual in Indiana's history".

More Books by Ryan Green

On 29th February 2000, John Price took out a restraining order against his girlfriend, Katherine Knight. Later that day, he told his co-workers that she had stabbed him and if he were ever to go missing, it was because Knight had killed him.

The next day, Price didn't show up for work.

A co-worker was sent to check on him. They found a bloody handprint by the front door and they immediately contacted the police. The local police force was not prepared for the chilling scene they were about to encounter.

Price's body was found in a chair, legs crossed, with a bottle of lemonade under his arm. He'd been decapitated and skinned. The "skin-suit" was hanging from a meat hook in the living room and his head was found in the kitchen, in a pot of vegetables that was still warm. There were two plates on the dining table, each had the name of one of Price's children on it. She was attempting to serve his body parts to his children.

More Books by Ryan Green

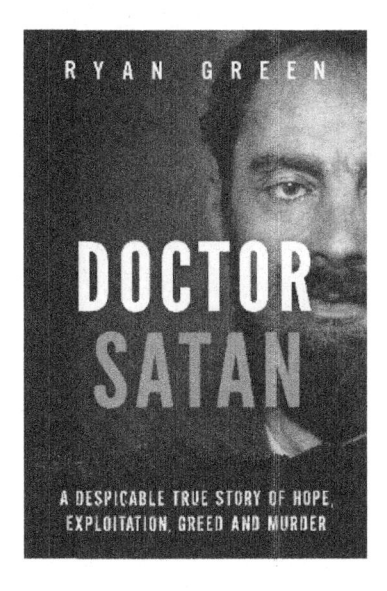

In 1944, as the Nazis occupied Paris, the French Police and Fire Brigade were called to investigate a vile-smelling smoke pouring out from a Parisian home. Inside, they were confronted with a scene from a nightmare. They found a factory line of bodies and multiple furnaces stocked with human remains.

When questioned, Dr. Petiot claimed that he was a part of the Resistance and the bodies they discovered belonged to Nazi collaborators that he killed for the cause. The French Police, resentful of Nazi occupation and confused by a rational alternative, allowed him to leave.

Was the respected Doctor a clandestine hero fighting for national liberty or a deviant using dire domestic circumstances to his advantage? One thing is for certain, the Police and the Nazis both wanted to get their hands on Dr. Marcel Petiot to find out the truth.

More Books by Ryan Green

In 1861, the police of a rural French village tore their way into the woodside home of Martin Dumollard. Inside, they found chaos. Paths had been carved through mounds of bloodstained clothing, reaching as high as the ceiling in some places.

The officers assumed that the mysterious maid-robber had killed one woman but failed in his other attempts. Yet, it was becoming sickeningly clear that there was a vast gulf between the crimes they were aware of and the ones that had truly been committed.

Would Dumollard's wife expose his dark secret or was she inextricably linked to the atrocities? Whatever the circumstances, everyone was desperate to discover whether the bloody garments belonged to some of the 648 missing women.

DISCOVER MORE FROM RYAN GREEN

Stay in the loop with the latest releases and exclusive offers by following Ryan!

Follow me:

Facebook   geni.us/ryangreenFB

Instagram   geni.us/ryangreenIG

Amazon   geni.us/ryangreenAM

www.ryangreenbooks.com

RYAN GREEN

Free True Crime Audiobook

Sign up to Audible and use your free credit to download this collection of twelve books. If you cancel within 30 days, there's no charge!

WWW.RYANGREENBOOKS.COM/FREE-AUDIOBOOK

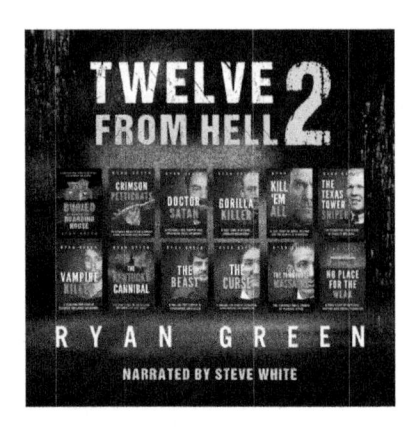

"Ryan Green has produced another excellent book and belongs at the top with true crime writers such as M. William Phelps, Gregg Olsen and Ann Rule" **–B.S. Reid**

"Wow! Chilling, shocking and totally riveting! I'm not going to sleep well after listening to this but the narration was fantastic. Crazy story but highly recommend for any true crime lover!" **–Mandy**

"Torture Mom by Ryan Green left me pretty speechless. The fact that it's a true story is just...wow" **–JStep**

"Graphic, upsetting, but superbly read and written" **–Ray C**

WWW.RYANGREENBOOKS.COM/FREE-AUDIOBOOK